ELECTROMAGNETIC PULSE (EMP): THREAT TO CRITICAL INFRASTRUCTURE

HEARING

BEFORE THE

SUBCOMMITTEE ON CYBERSECURITY, INFRASTRUCTURE PROTECTION, AND SECURITY TECHNOLOGIES

OF THE

COMMITTEE ON HOMELAND SECURITY HOUSE OF REPRESENTATIVES

ONE HUNDRED THIRTEENTH CONGRESS

SECOND SESSION

MAY 8, 2014

Serial No. 113-68

Printed for the use of the Committee on Homeland Security

Available via the World Wide Web: http://www.gpo.gov/fdsys/

U.S. GOVERNMENT PRINTING OFFICE

89-763 PDF   WASHINGTON : 2014

For sale by the Superintendent of Documents, U.S. Government Printing Office
Internet: bookstore.gpo.gov   Phone: toll free (866) 512-1800; DC area (202) 512-1800
Fax: (202) 512-2250   Mail: Stop SSOP, Washington, DC 20402-0001

COMMITTEE ON HOMELAND SECURITY

MICHAEL T. MCCAUL, Texas, *Chairman*

LAMAR SMITH, Texas
PETER T. KING, New York
MIKE ROGERS, Alabama
PAUL C. BROUN, Georgia
CANDICE S. MILLER, Michigan, *Vice Chair*
PATRICK MEEHAN, Pennsylvania
JEFF DUNCAN, South Carolina
TOM MARINO, Pennsylvania
JASON CHAFFETZ, Utah
STEVEN M. PALAZZO, Mississippi
LOU BARLETTA, Pennsylvania
RICHARD HUDSON, North Carolina
STEVE DAINES, Montana
SUSAN W. BROOKS, Indiana
SCOTT PERRY, Pennsylvania
MARK SANFORD, South Carolina
VACANCY

BENNIE G. THOMPSON, Mississippi
LORETTA SANCHEZ, California
SHEILA JACKSON LEE, Texas
YVETTE D. CLARKE, New York
BRIAN HIGGINS, New York
CEDRIC L. RICHMOND, Louisiana
WILLIAM R. KEATING, Massachusetts
RON BARBER, Arizona
DONDALD M. PAYNE, JR., New Jersey
BETO O'ROURKE, Texas
FILEMON VELA, Texas
ERIC SWALWELL, California
VACANCY
VACANCY

BRENDAN P. SHIELDS, *Staff Director*
MICHAEL GEFFROY, *Deputy Staff Director/Chief Counsel*
MICHAEL S. TWINCHEK, *Chief Clerk*
I. LANIER AVANT, *Minority Staff Director*

SUBCOMMITTEE ON CYBERSECURITY, INFRASTRUCTURE PROTECTION, AND SECURITY TECHNOLOGIES

PATRICK MEEHAN, Pennsylvania, *Chairman*

MIKE ROGERS, Alabama
TOM MARINO, Pennsylvania
JASON CHAFFETZ, Utah
STEVE DAINES, Montana
SCOTT PERRY, Pennsylvania, *Vice Chair*
MICHAEL T. MCCAUL, Texas *(ex officio)*

YVETTE D. CLARKE, New York
WILLIAM R. KEATING, Massachusetts
FILEMON VELA, Texas
VACANCY
BENNIE G. THOMPSON, Mississippi *(ex officio)*

ALEX MANNING, *Subcommittee Staff Director*
DENNIS TERRY, *Subcommittee Clerk*

CONTENTS

ELECTROMAGNETIC PULSE (EMP): THREAT TO CRITICAL INFRASTRUCTURE

Thursday, May 8, 2014

U.S. House of Representatives,
Committee on Homeland Security,
Subcommittee on Cybersecurity, Infrastructure
Protection, and Security Technologies,
Washington, DC.

The subcommittee met, pursuant to call, at 2:03 p.m., in Room 311, Cannon House Office Building, Hon. Scott Perry presiding.

Present: Representatives Perry, McCaul (ex officio), Clarke, and Vela.

Also present: Representative Franks.

Mr. PERRY. Ladies and gentlemen, the Committee on Homeland Security, Subcommittee on Cybersecurity, Infrastructure Protection, and Security Technologies will come to order. The subcommittee is meeting today to examine the threats to critical infrastructure posed by electromagnetic pulse, or EMP.

Before we begin today's hearing, I ask unanimous consent that Congressman Franks be permitted to participate in today's hearing, and, without objection, so ordered.

At this time I would like to recognize the Chairman for a brief set of opening remarks.

Mr. MCCAUL. I thank the Chairman and Mr. Perry for his leadership in chairing this committee hearing, Ms. Clarke as well. I just got back from the World War II memorial service. I spoke, talked about my father, who was a World War II veteran, bombardier. I mention that not to talk about my dad, but because this issue really goes back to the advent of the nuclear age, and it is an issue that the American people really don't know much about. They are not familiar with this issue.

Some would say it is a low probability, but the damage that could be caused in the event of an EMP attack both by the sun, a solar event, or a man-made attack would be catastrophic. We talk a lot about a nuclear bomb in Manhattan, and we talk about a cybersecurity threat, the grid, power grid, in the Northeast, and all these things would actually probably pale in comparison to the devastation that an EMP attack could perpetrate on Americans.

We have extraordinary capability in this country to do great things. We are a responsible Nation with our power and with our might. But a nation, a rogue nation, with that type of capability in the wrong hands could be devastating.

Again, I want to commend the Chairman. I want to commend Congressman Franks for his leadership. I don't think any Member of Congress knows this issue more than he does, and I know your testimony in the record will be very valuable as we look at developing legislation to deal with this very critical and important issue to our National security.

With that, Mr. Chairman. I yield back.

Mr. PERRY. Thank you, Mr. Chairman.

I recognize myself at this time for an opening statement.

I would like to thank everyone for attending today. Chairman Meehan is unable to attend, but as Vice Chairman of this subcommittee, I am honored and privileged and pleased to chair this important hearing on the threat and consequences to our Nation's critical infrastructure from electromagnetic pulse, EMP.

In 1962, the United States conducted a test named STARFISH Prime where the military detonated a 1.4-megaton thermonuclear bomb about 25 miles above Johnston Atoll in the in the Pacific. In space, six American, British, and Soviet satellites suffered damage, and 800 miles away in Hawaii, burglar alarms sounded, street lights blinked out, and phones, radios, and televisions went dead. While only 1 percent of the existing street lights were affected, it became clear that electromagnetic pulse, or EMP, could cause significant damage.

EMP is simply a burst of electromagnetic radiation that results from certain types of high-energy explosions or from a suddenly fluctuating magnetic field. A frightening point is that EMP can be generated by nuclear weapons, from naturally-occurring sources such as solar storms, or specialized non-nuclear EMP weapons.

Nuclear weapon EMPs are most catastrophic when a nuclear weapon is detonated at a high altitude at approximately 30 kilometers, or 20 miles, above the intended target. The consequences of such an attack could be catastrophic. All electronics, I mention all electronics, power systems, and information systems could be shut down. This could then cascade into interdependent infrastructure such as water, gas, and telecommunications. While we understand that this is an extreme case, we must always be prepared in case a rogue state decides to utilize this technology.

Now, currently the nations of Russia and China have the technology to launch an EMP attack, and we have speculated that Iran and North Korea may be developing EMP weapon technology. This is why we must remain vigilant in our efforts to mitigate the effects of an EMP attack.

Since most critical infrastructure, particularly electrical infrastructure, is in the hands of private owners, the Federal Government has limited authority to mandate preparedness. While some people criticize the lack of DHS action on compelling the private sector to harden their systems against EMP, it is important to note that DHS has no statutory authority whatsoever to regulate the electric grid. My hope is that this hearing will be successful in educating the public on the threat of EMP and will alleviate some of the fears that people have on EMP attacks.

I thank the witnesses at this time for their time and look forward to their testimony.

[The statement of Vice Chairman Perry follows:]

STATEMENT OF VICE CHAIRMAN SCOTT PERRY

I would like to thank everyone for attending today. Chairman Meehan is unable to attend but as Vice Chairman of this subcommittee, I am honored and pleased to chair this important hearing on the threat and consequences to our Nation's critical infrastructure from Electromagnetic Pulse (EMP).

In 1962 the United States conducted a test named STARFISH PRIME, where the military detonated a 1.4 megaton thermonuclear bomb about 25 miles above Johnston Atoll in the Pacific. In space, six American, British, and Soviet satellites suffered damage and 800 miles away in Hawaii, burglar alarms sounded, street lights blinked out, and phones, radios, and televisions went dead. While only 1% of the existing street lights were affected, it became clear that electromagnetic pulse, or EMP, could cause significant damage.

EMP is simply a burst of electromagnetic radiation that results from certain types of high-energy explosions or from a suddenly fluctuating magnetic field. A frightening point is that EMP can be generated by nuclear weapons, from naturally-occurring sources such as solar storms, or specialized non-nuclear EMP weapons. Nuclear weapon EMPs are most catastrophic when a nuclear weapon is detonated at high altitude, at approximately 30 kilometers (20 miles), above the intended target. The consequences of such an attack could be catastrophic; all electronics, power systems, and information systems could be shut down. This could then cascade into interdependent infrastructures such as water, gas, and telecommunications. While we understand this is an extreme case, we must always be prepared in case a rouge state decides to utilize this technology.

Currently, the nations of Russia and China have the technology to launch an EMP attack, and we have speculated that Iran and North Korea may be developing EMP weapon technology. This is why we must remain vigilant in our efforts to mitigate the effects of an EMP attack. Since most critical infrastructure, particularly electrical infrastructure, is in the hands of private owners, the Federal Government has limited authority to mandate preparedness. While some people criticize the lack of DRS action on compelling the private sector to harden their systems against EMP, it is important to note that DRS has no statutory authority whatsoever to regulate the electric grid.

My hope is that this hearing will be successful in educating the public on the threat of EMP and will alleviate some of the fears that people have on EMP attacks. I thank the witnesses for their time and look forward to their testimony.

Mr. PERRY. At this time the Chairman now recognizes the Ranking Member of the subcommittee, the gentlelady from New York, Ms. Clarke for a statement she may have.

Ms. CLARKE. Thank you, Mr. Vice Chairman, and welcome to the gavel, and thank you for chairing this hearing on electromagnetic pulse and the threat to our critical infrastructure today.

I, too, want to extend a warm welcome in return to our colleague Congressman Franks to our subcommittee. I believe that the last time you testified before us was back in 2012. Congressman Franks and I co-chaired the EMP Caucus here in Congress. Though we are from different ends of the continent, we share a concern about the vulnerability and resiliency of our Nation's critical infrastructure.

I also want to welcome back Dr. Chris Beck, who will appear on Panel II. He was my past subcommittee director, and it is good to see.

I am very interested in the testimony today and hoping to hear about how we can assess the risk of solar geomagnetic storms and other EMP threats that create vulnerabilities for our critical infrastructure. Since we know the electric grid is vulnerable to physical natural threats like heavy weather, EMPs from solar weather, and malicious cyber threats, it is important for the subcommittee to have a fuller understanding of the threats.

As I see it, the main risk from a terrorist attack succeeding against the electric power industry would be a widespread power outage that lasted for an extended period of time. The most critical components of the transmission system are the high-voltage and extra-high-voltage transformers, or EHVs, but we must not forget the other major components of the electric transmission system that are vulnerable to terrorist attack: The transmission lines, transmission towers, and control centers.

Utilities rarely experience loss of an individual EHV transformer, but recovery from such a loss takes months, especially if no spare is available. Conversely, utilities regularly experience damage to transmission towers and substations due to weather and malicious activities and are able to recover from this damage fairly rapidly.

Experts generally agree that a failure, for whatever reason, involving several key EHV transformers could cause blackouts lasting weeks and deteriorated service for an area that could last months, and that the economic consequences of such an attack would likely be large.

We also know that public-private partnerships are the keystone to solving this challenge, especially because the large majority of our electric grid is privately held by investor-owned utilities, or they are part of the rural electric cooperatives network, utilities owned by their member customers in 47 States, or the public power municipal utilities.

The Electric Power Research Institute, or EPRI, an industry-funded energy research consortium, is also addressing high-voltage transformer vulnerabilities, and in cooperation with the North American Electric Reliability Corporation, EPRI has been developing conceptual designs for recovery transformers which would enable rapid temporary replacement of damaged high-voltage transformers. High-voltage and extra-high-voltage transformers are very large, extremely difficult to transport, and, until 2009, primarily manufactured overseas, complicating rapid recovery and restoration efforts.

The Department of Homeland Security has a variety of efforts for EMP and all-hazards risks including research on technologies to improve resiliency in the electric grid corridor. The DHS Science and Technology Directorate has co-sponsored with private utilities an exercise and a fast turnaround transformer replacement project. This effort is known as the Recovery Transformer Project, or RecX, and it hopes to increase the resiliency of the transmission power grid through the use of more mobile and modular transformers.

This applied research effort has developed a prototype EHV transformer that can quickly be deployed to a site via a series of large trucks and trailers and then installed, assembled, and energized rapidly. The prototype RecX was demonstrated last year and installed in the grid at a host utility, and it is currently undergoing a 1-year observational period to verify its performance.

However, within DHS, identifying specific EMP-threat-related programs in their budgets is difficult because EMP-specific preparedness and response is not the primary purpose of most programs generally characterized as all-hazards threats. Some see this as a problem; however, under the current sequester budgetary constraints, funding sources for mitigation and response preparedness for low-probability risk compete directly with today's on-the-ground first-responder needs.

Unfortunately EMP events of all sorts have become the darling of the internet and late-night talk radio, forecasting "the end of civilization as we know it" conditions. They include all kinds of lurid descriptions of hypothetical catastrophic social events that will, without any doubt in their minds, occur when an EMP event happens, according to these soothsayers. It can be disturbing.

EMP-related events have even been popularized in melodramatic TV shows. Books of science fiction have popularized EMP end-of-day scenarios; and, of course, the internet has innumerable EMP sites that tout the devastation to come.

Since I have been on this committee, I and others have been careful not to use our positions of influence to promote fear in the public. While the threat of an EMP event is real, I believe we need to use scientific, risk-based, and, frankly, common-sense plans and exercises to give us a clearer picture of how to prevent and respond in the event of an EMP incident. More complete understanding of preparedness, response, and recovery activities related to any type of EMP incident could provide a thoughtful background that can assist the Nation's resiliency if high-impact EMP events do occur.

I look forward to the testimony today, and I yield back the balance of my time.

[The statement of Ranking Member Clarke follows:]

STATEMENT OF RANKING MEMBER YVETTE D. CLARKE

MAY 8, 2014

I'm very interested in the testimony today, and hoping to hear about how we can assess the risk of solar geomagnetic storms and other EMP threats that create vulnerabilities for our critical infrastructure.

Since we know the electric grid is vulnerable to physical natural threats like heavy weather, EMPs from solar weather, and malicious cyber threats, it is important for the subcommittee to have a fuller understanding of the threats.

As I see it, the main risk from a terrorist attack succeeding against the electric power industry would be a widespread power outage that lasted for an extended period of time.

The most critical components of the transmission system are the High-Voltage and Extra-High-Voltage transformers, or EHVs. But we must not forget the other major components of the electric transmission system that are vulnerable to terrorist attack—the transmission lines, transmission towers, and control centers.

Utilities rarely experience loss of an individual EHV transformer, but recovery from such a loss takes months, especially if no spare is available.

Conversely, utilities regularly experience damage to transmission towers and substations due to both weather and malicious activities, and are able to recover from this damage fairly rapidly.

Experts generally agree that a failure, for whatever reason, involving several key EHV transformers, could cause blackouts lasting weeks and deteriorated service for an area that could last months, and that the economic consequences of such an attack would likely be large.

We also know that public/private partnerships are the keystone to solving this challenge, especially because the large majority of our electric grid is privately held by investor-owned utilities, or they are part of the Rural Electric Cooperatives network, utilities owned by their member-customers in 47 States, or the Public Power municipal utilities.

The Electric Power Research Institute, or EPRI, an industry-funded energy research consortium, is also addressing High-Voltage transformer vulnerabilities, and in cooperation with the North American Electric Reliability Corporation, EPRI has been developing conceptual designs for "recovery transformers" which would enable rapid temporary replacement of damaged High-Voltage transformers.

High-Voltage and Extra-High-Voltage transformers are very large, extremely difficult to transport, and until 2009 primarily manufactured overseas, complicating rapid recovery and restoration efforts.

The Department of Homeland Security has a variety of efforts for EMP and "all-hazards risks", including research on technologies to improve resiliency in the electric grid sector.

The DHS Science & Technology Directorate has co-sponsored with private utilities an exercise in a fast turnaround transformer replacement project.

This effort is known as the Recovery Transformer Project, or RecX, and it hopes to increase the resiliency of the transmission power grid through the use of more mobile and modular transformers.

This applied research effort has developed a prototype EHV transformer that can quickly be deployed to a site via a series of large trucks and trailers, and then installed, assembled, and energized rapidly.

The prototype RecX was demonstrated last year, and installed in the grid at a host utility, and it is currently undergoing a 1-year observational period to verify its performance.

However, within DHS, identifying specific EMP threat-related programs and their budgets is difficult, because EMP-specific preparedness and response is not the primary purpose of most programs generally characterized as "all-hazards threats." Some see this as a problem.

However, under the current sequester budgetary constraints, funding sources for mitigation and response preparedness for low probability risks, compete directly with today's on-the-ground first responder needs.

Unfortunately, EMP events of all sorts have become the darling of the internet and late-night talk radio forecasting "end of civilization as we know it" conditions.

They include all kinds of lurid descriptions of hypothetical catastrophic social events that will, without any doubt in their minds, occur when an EMP event happens, according to these soothsayers.

It can be disturbing. EMP related events have even been popularized in melodramatic TV shows. Books of science fiction have popularized EMP end-of-days scenarios, and of course, the internet has innumerable EMP sites that tout the devastation to come.

Since I have been on this committee, I, and others, have been careful not to use our positions of influence to promote fear in the public.

While the threat of an EMP event is real, I believe we need to use scientific, risk-based, and frankly, common-sense plans and exercises to give us a clearer picture of how to prevent and respond in the event of an EMP incident.

A more complete understanding of preparedness, response, and recovery activities related to any type of EMP incident, could provide a thoughtful background that can assist the Nation's resiliency, if high-impact EMP events do occur.

Mr. PERRY. The Vice Chairman thanks the Ranking Member.

Other Members of the committee are reminded that opening statements may be submitted for the record.

[The statement of Ranking Member Thompson follows:]

STATEMENT OF RANKING MEMBER BENNIE G. THOMPSON

Scientists tell us that it is likely that a powerful geomagnetic solar storm, capable of affecting parts of the U.S. and Canadian electrical grid could occur. When it will occur, we are not quite sure.

What we do know is that last year, 2013 was forecasted as the next period of elevated solar activity, known as "solar maximum", and we are in a high-activity part of a cyclical process.

The popularity of an EMP event occurring in the United States has taken on the dimensions of a doomsday—end of civilization as we know it—scenario, and it includes all sorts of catastrophic events surrounding possible solar storms, and other kinds of EMP attacks.

These stories are rampant throughout current media—fiction books have been popularized about it, the internet has innumerable sites that tout the devastation to come, and it is the subject of late-night talk radio regularly.

Since I have been on this committee, I have urged my colleagues not to use our positions of influence to promote fear in the public.

While the threat of an EMP event is real, I believe we need to use common-sense, risk-based scenarios and exercises to give us a picture of how to prevent or respond to an EMP event.

Many blame the current administration for their frustrations about EMP. However, no one from the Federal Government is here today to testify about the issue.

Today, we will not hear from Government specialists and experts from the Department of Energy or Homeland Security on this issue.

It is the responsibility of this committee to know the probability of such an event, and the likelihood and severity of the effects on the electric grid and other critical infrastructure.

What's important to me is that in this time of increasingly tight budgets, and the current sequester budget for homeland security, we must depend on sophisticated risk analysis to guide us in making the tough decisions about our spending priorities.

Furthermore, we need to explore how we can leverage this risk analysis to sensibly prioritize our spending and especially make use of the existing public/private partnerships to deal with such a threat.

Mr. PERRY. We are pleased to have two distinguished panels of witness before us today on this important topic. The Honorable Trent Franks represents Arizona's Eighth Congressional District, serving in Congress since 2003. Prior to coming to Washington, Representative Franks was president of Liberty Petroleum Corporation, a small oil exploration company established in 1996. He had previously held positions in the Arizona State Legislature and in the Governor's Office for Children.

Since coming to Congress, Representative Franks has been an advocate for robust preparation against a potential EMP event, natural or man-made. He launched the Congressional EMP Caucus and has pushed for passage of the Secure High-Voltage Infrastructure for Electricity from Lethal Damage Act, or the SHIELD Act.

Thanks for being here. Your full written statement will appear in the record. The Chairman now recognizes Mr. Franks for his testimony.

STATEMENT OF HON. TRENT FRANKS, A REPRESENTATIVE IN CONGRESS FROM THE STATE OF ARIZONA

Mr. FRANKS. Good afternoon, Chairman Perry, and Ranking Member Clarke, and fellow distinguished Members on the committee. I believe the subject of this hearing today is one of profound implication and importance to our country, and I am very grateful to you for allowing me to testify.

Mr. Chairman and Members of the committee, America is so reliant on our electric grid that we specifically consider it, "critical infrastructure." With each passing year our society becomes increasingly dependent on technology and an abundant supply of electricity. Our household appliances, food-distribution systems, telephone and computer networks, our communication devices, water and sewage plants would all grind to a halt without electric power.

At the same time, the use of modern computerized control systems along with the increased size and integration of our grid has made it far more vulnerable to electromagnetic pulse or geomagnetic disturbance than ever before. Consequently, nearly every single facet of modern human life in America is now susceptible to being crippled by a major natural or man-made EMP event, and nearly every space, weather, and EMP expert recognizes the dramatic disruptions and cataclysmic collapses these pulses can potentially bring to electric grids.

In 2004 and 2008, the EMP Commission, which some of the members of that will be here today, testified before those of us on the Armed Services Committee that the U.S. society and economy are so critically dependent upon the availability of electricity that a significant collapse of the grid precipitated by a major natural or man-made event, EMP or otherwise, could result in catastrophic civilian casualties. Let me say that again. Could result in cata-strophic civilian casualties. That conclusion is echoed by separate reports recently compiled by the Department of Defense, Department of Homeland Security, Department of Energy, the National Academy of Sciences, along with various other Government agencies and independent researchers.

We now have 11 Governmental agencies' studies on the severe threat and vulnerabilities we face from EMP and GMD, all of which came to very similar conclusions. In fact, you should have in front of you booklets both from the Center for Security Policy and the Heritage Foundation that give some insight into some of these studies.

We as a Nation have spent billions of dollars over several decades hardening our nuclear triad, our missile defense capabilities, and numerous other critical elements of our National security apparatus against the effects of electromagnetic pulse, particularly the type of electromagnetic pulse that might be deliberately generated against us by an enemy; however, our civilian grid upon which the Department of Defense relies upon for nearly 99 percent of its electricity needs, is completely vulnerable to the same kind of danger. Mr. Chairman, our enemies are actually and acutely aware of that vulnerability, and it constitutes, in my opinion, an invitation to them to use the asymmetric capacity of an EMP weapon against us should they choose to do so.

To address this National security threat, Chairman Pete Sessions and I have introduced the Critical Infrastructure Protection Act, H.R. 3410, which is now before your committee, and we would like to specifically thank Ranking Member Yvette Clarke for co-sponsoring this critical legislation. H.R. 3410 enhances the Department of Homeland Security's threat assessments for geomagnetic disturbances and electromagnetic pulse blackouts, which will enable practical steps to protect the electric grid that serves our Nation. This legislation will also help the United States prepare for such an event by including potential large-scale extended blackouts into existing National planning scenarios. It allows us to plan for protecting and recovering the electric grid and other critical infrastructure from an EMP event. Perhaps most importantly, Mr. Chairman, it advances an awareness program to educate and, I hope, motivate all of us inside and outside of Government to proactively protect against this potentially devastating danger to our country.

In closing, Mr. Chairman, let me suggest to you all that there is a moment in the life of nearly every problem when it is big enough to be seen and still small enough to be addressed. I believe we now live in that moment as it relates to the threat of natural or weaponized EMP.

The challenge to ultimately and comprehensively protect our people and Nation from all of the various perils of natural or man-made EMP will be long and lingering, but the time to protect our Nation from the most devastating scenario is now. The threat is real, and the implications are profoundly sobering. Your actions today to protect America may gain you no fame or fanfare in the annals of history; however, it may happen in your lifetime that a natural or man-made EMP event so big has an effect so small that no one but a few will recognize the disaster that was averted, and for the sake of our children and future generations, I pray it happens exactly that way.

I thank you, and God bless you all.

[The prepared statement of Mr. Franks follows:]

STATEMENT OF HON. TRENT FRANKS

Good afternoon Chairman Perry, Ranking Member Clarke, and fellow distinguished Members on the committee. I believe the subject of this hearing is one of profound implication and importance and consequently I am grateful to you all for allowing me to testify here today.

With each passing year, our society becomes increasingly dependent on technology and an abundant supply of electricity. Our entire American way of life relies upon electrical power and technology. Our household appliances, food-distribution systems, telephone and computer networks, communication devices, water and sewage plants would grind to a halt without it. Nearly every single facet of modern human life in America is susceptible to being crippled by a major Electromagnetic Pulse or Geomagnetic Disturbance event. We are so reliant on our electric power grid that we specifically consider it "critical infrastructure".

Mr. Chairman and Members of the committee, it strikes at my very core when I think of the men, women, and children in cities and rural towns across America with a possibility of no access to food, water, or transportation. In a matter of weeks or months at most, a worst-case scenario could bring devastation beyond imagination.

The effects of geomagnetic storms and electromagnetic pulses on electric infrastructure are well-documented, with nearly every space, weather, and EMP expert recognizing the dramatic disruptions and cataclysmic collapses these pulses can bring to electric grids. In 2008, the EMP Commission testified before The Armed Services Committee, of which I am a member, that the U.S. society and economy are so critically dependent upon the availability of electricity that a significant collapse of the grid, precipitated by a major natural or man-made EMP event, could result in catastrophic civilian casualties. This conclusion is echoed by separate reports recently compiled by the DOD, DHS, DOE, NAS, along with various other Government agencies and independent researchers. All came to very similar conclusions. We now have 11 Government studies on the severe threat and vulnerabilities we face from EMP and GMD.

RECENT EVENTS

Mr. Chairman, as you can see, we have known the potentially devastating effects of sufficiently intense electromagnetic pulse on the electronic systems and its risk to our National security. More troubling, our enemies know.

More than a year ago, an unknown number of shooters with AK–47s knocked out 17 large transformers during a highly-choreographed assault on the PG&E Metcalf Transmission Substation in California. While the power company was able to avoid blackouts, the damage to the facility took nearly 4 weeks to repair.

This is not an isolated incident and world-wide adversaries are taking notice in the vulnerability of our grid. Just last month, Connecticut officials released a report discussing their efforts to protect utility and distribution companies because hackers and cyber attackers around the world have made attempts to penetrate their systems.

THE THREATS

We as a Nation have spent billions of dollars over the years hardening our nuclear triad, our missile-defense capabilities, and numerous other critical elements of our National security apparatus against the effects of electromagnetic pulse, particularly the type of electromagnetic pulse that might be generated against us by an enemy. However, our civilian grid, which the Defense Department relies upon for nearly 99% of its electricity needs, is completely vulnerable to the same kind of danger. This constitutes an invitation on the part of certain enemies of the United States to use the asymmetric capability of an EMP weapon against us.

We also face the threat of a natural EMP event. Since the last occurrence of a major geomagnetic storm in 1921, the Nation's high-voltage and extra-high-voltage systems have increased in size more than ten-fold. We are currently entering an interval of increased solar activity and are likely to encounter an increasing number of geomagnetic events on earth.

LEGISLATION

To this end, I introduced The Critical Infrastructure Protection Act, H.R. 3410, which currently lays before your committee. I'd like to thank Ranking Member Clarke, and my EMP Caucus co-chair for cosponsoring this critical legislation. H.R. 3410 enhances the Department of Homeland Security's threat assessments for geomagnetic disturbances and electromagnetic pulse blackouts which will enable practical steps to protect the electric grid that serves our Nation. This legislation will also help the United States prepare for such an event by implementing large-scale blackouts into existing National planning scenarios. It allows us to plan for protecting and recovering the electric grid and other critical infrastructure from an EMP event. In addition, it advances an educational awareness program to protect critical infrastructure and constructs a campaign to proactively educate emergency planners and emergency responders at all levels of government.

SUMMARY

Mr. Chairman, the challenge to ultimately and fully protect our people and Nation from all of the various perils of natural or man-made electromagnetic pulse will be long and lingering. But the time to protect our Nation from the most devastating scenario is now; the threat is real, and the implications are sobering.

Your actions today to protect America may gain you no fame or fanfare in the annals of history. However, it may happen in your lifetime that a natural or man-made EMP event so big has an effect so small that no one but a few will recognize the disaster that was averted. For the sake of our children and future generations, I pray it happens exactly that way.

Thank you and God bless all of you. Thank you and I yield back the balance of my time.

Mr. PERRY. The Chairman thanks Representative Franks and welcomes you to the dais at this time.

Mr. FRANKS. Were there any questions, Mr. Chairman?

Mr. PERRY. Are there any questions, Ms. Clarke? We don't have any questions at this point.

Mr. FRANKS. I would then also refer you once again to the materials that we brought to the committee.

Mr. PERRY. Absolutely. If the other panel will be seated. While they are doing so, I ask unanimous consent to enter into the record a statement by Rules Committee Chairman Pete Sessions, who wanted to attend this hearing today, but was delayed on the floor. Without objection.

[The statement of Mr. Sessions follows:]

STATEMENT OF HON. PETE SESSIONS

Last month's anniversary of the attacks on the Metcalf Power Station remind us that attacks on key elements of the Nation's bulk power distribution system—popularly known as the "electric grid"—have exposed a serious lack of resiliency in this critical infrastructure. We are on notice that, if as a result, the power was to be disrupted for protracted periods; the consequences could be nothing short of catastrophic.

Mr. Chairman, I thank you and the subcommittee for holding this hearing to address what is arguably the most serious of the threats to the grid: The possibility that a single nuclear weapon detonated in space high over this country could unleash intense electromagnetic pulses (EMP), disrupting for many months—if not indefinitely—the supply of power to large area.

Until recently, information about EMP was Classified and many of us have little knowledge of the serious danger such threats represents to everything we hold dear.

Unfortunately, even if those who wish to do this country harm know about our grid's vulnerability to EMP choose not to exploit it, the bulk power distribution system will be subjected to effects similar to what are known as the E–3 pulses caused by nuclear detonations in space.

Roughly every 150 years, the sun emits in the earth's direction an intense coronal mass ejection, or solar flare, that can severely damage or destroy unprotected electronic devices and electric systems. Such solar storms are known as "Carrington

Events," named for the scientist who first identified the phenomenon when it last occurred in 1859—155 years ago.

Whatever its source, the consequences of such electromagnetic pulses could be devastating for many millions of people who would be left without access to potable water, food, bank accounts, medications, communications, transportation, and many other important electronically-based activities—possibly for the indefinite future.

Dr. William Graham, the chairman of the EMP Threat Commission, believes that, if the power goes out and stays out for even 1 year's time, as many as 9 out of 10 of us would perish.

Fortunately, Mr. Chairman, we need not face such a horrific prospect. We know how to protect electrical and electronic devices from the effects of EMP. In fact, the Department of Defense has been doing it with respect to the military's nuclear deterrent and command-and-control systems for over 50 years.

There are, in short, proven and easily implementable techniques that can now be applied to ensure the resilience ofthe U.S. electric grid and the things that depend upon it in 21st Century America—which is just about everything.

A first step towards such corrective action would be for the adoption ofthe Critical Infrastructure Protection Act (CIPA), H.R. 3410. It will require the Department of Homeland Security to make EMP one of its National planning scenarios. This legislation represents the first step toward raising awareness about the gravity of the threats to our grid and the other critical infrastructures that depend upon it.

I commend the subcommittee for focusing on this potentially existential danger and urge your Members to give early and favorable consideration to the CIPA.

Mr. PERRY. Thank you, gentlemen. I will start with introductions.

Dr. Peter Vincent Pry is the executive director of the Task Force on National and Homeland Security, a Congressional advisory board dedicated to achieving protection of the United States from electromagnetic pulse and other threats. Dr. Pry is also the director of the United States Nuclear Strategy Forum, an advisory body to Congress on policies to counter weapons of mass destruction. Dr. Pry has served on the staffs of the Congressional Commission on the Strategic Posture of the United States, the Commission to Assess the Threat to the U.S. from an EMP Attack, the House Armed Services Committee, as an intelligence officer with the CIA, and as a verification analyst at the U.S. Arms Control and Disarmament Agency.

Dr. Michael Frankel is a senior scientist at the Penn State—and I must pause for a moment. We are, just in case you are wondering who I am, where I went to school—at the Penn State University Applied Physics Laboratory, and one of the Nation's leading experts on the effects of nuclear weapons. Formerly he served as the executive director of the Congressional Commission to Assess the Threat to the U.S. from EMP, and as the chief science officer for L–3 Communications. In prior Government service, Dr. Frankel served various National security capacities, including with the Office of Advanced Energetics and Nuclear Weapons at the Department of Defense, the Nuclear Phenomenology Division at the Defense Threat Reduction Agency, and as a research physicist at the Naval Surface Weapons Center. Also known for his expertise in directed energy and advanced energetic materials, he has made seminal contributions to key strategic defense programs and has been active in international scientific exchanges.

Dr. Chris Beck is the vice president for policy and strategic initiatives for the Electric Infrastructure Security Council. Dr. Beck is a technical and policy expert in several homeland security and National defense-related areas, including critical infrastructure protection, science and technology development, WMD prevention and protection, and emerging threat identification. Dr. Beck served on the staff of the House Committee on Homeland Security, as well as a staffer for Congresswoman Loretta Sanchez. Before Government service, Dr. Beck was a post-doctoral fellow and adjunct professor at Northeastern University.

Thank you all for being here. The full written statements of witnesses will appear in the record, and at this time the Chairman recognizes Dr. Pry for 5 minutes for his testimony.

STATEMENT OF PETER VINCENT PRY, CONGRESSIONAL EMP COMMISSION, CONGRESSIONAL STRATEGIC POSTURE COMMISSION, AND EXECUTIVE DIRECTOR OF THE TASK FORCE ON NATIONAL AND HOMELAND SECURITY

Mr. PRY. Thank you for this opportunity to testify at your hearing on the threat posed by electromagnetic pulse to critical infrastructure.

Natural EMP from a geomagnetic super-storm like the 1859 Carrington Event or the 1921 Railroad Storm, a nuclear EMP attack from terrorists or rogue states as practiced by North Korea during the nuclear crisis of 2013 are both existential threats that could kill 9 of 10 Americans through starvation, disease, and societal collapse.

A natural EMP catastrophe or nuclear EMP attack could black out the National electric grid for months or years and collapse all the other critical infrastructures, communications, transportation, banking and finance, food and water, necessary to sustain modern society and the lives of 310 million Americans.

Passage of the SHIELD Act to protect the National electric grid is urgently necessary. In 2010, after the House unanimously passed the GRID Act, if one Senator had not put a hold on the bill, today in 2014 the Nation would already be protected since it would take about 3½ years to harden the grid. Passage of the Critical Infrastructure Protection Act, H.R. 3410, to create a new National planning scenario focused on EMP is urgently necessary. As the National planning scenarios are the basis for all Federal, State, and local emergency planning, training, and resource allocation, an EMP National planning scenario would immediately and significantly improve National preparedness for an EMP catastrophe.

The single most important thing Congress could do to protect the American people from EMP and from all the other threats to critical infrastructures is pass the Critical Infrastructure Protect Act, which bill is soon or will be before this committee for consideration.

Thousands of emergency planners and first responders at the Federal, State, and local level want to protect our Nation and their States and communities from the EMP threat, but they are seriously hindered and even prohibited from doing so because the EMP threat is not among the 15 canonical National planning scenarios utilized by the Department of Homeland Security.

Passage of the Critical Infrastructure Protection Act would immediately mobilize thousands of emergency planners and first responders at all levels of government and educate millions of others about the EMP threat and how to prepare for it.

Passage of the Critical Infrastructure Protection Act would immediately help States that are frustrated with the lack of action on

EMP in Washington and are trying to launch initiatives protecting their electrical grids from EMP, as is being attempted now in Maine, Virginia, Oklahoma, and Florida.

Passage of the Critical Infrastructure Protection Act would educate all States about the EMP threat and help them protect their critical infrastructures. For example, projects in New York and Massachusetts to harden their State grids against severe weather caused by climate change should include protection against an EMP event, which is the worst threat to the grid. If the grid is protected against EMP, it will mitigate all lesser threats, including cyber attack, sabotage, and severe weather.

Given the amounts of money being spent in New York and Massachusetts on grid hardening against severe weather, significant EMP protection can probably be accomplished now within their current budgets, but the cost of EMP protection will increase significantly if they delay and attempt remediation later.

EMP is a clear and present danger. A Carrington-class coronal mass ejection narrowly missed the earth in July 2012. Last April, during the nuclear crisis with North Korea over Kim Jong-Un's threatened nuclear strikes against the United States, Pyongyang apparently practiced an EMP attack with its KSM–3 satellite that passed over the U.S. heartland and over the Washington, D.C.-New York City corridor. Iran, estimated to be within 2 months of nuclear weapons by the administration, has a demonstrated capability to launch an EMP attack from a vessel at sea. The Iranian Revolutionary Guard Navy commenced patrols off the East Coast of the United States in February.

Thank you for your attention to EMP, which is the least understood but gravest threat to our society. This concludes my remarks.

[The prepared statement of Mr. Pry follows:]

PREPARED STATEMENT OF PETER VINCENT PRY

MAY 8, 2014

Thank you for this opportunity to testify at your hearing on the threat posed by electromagnetic pulse (EMP) to critical infrastructure.

Natural EMP from a geomagnetic super-storm, like the 1859 Carrington Event or 1921 Railroad Storm, and nuclear EMP attack from terrorists or rogue states, as practiced by North Korea during the nuclear crisis of 2013, are both existential threats that could kill 9 of 10 Americans through starvation, disease, and societal collapse.

A natural EMP catastrophe or nuclear EMP attack could blackout the National electric grid for months or years and collapse all the other critical infrastructures—communications, transportation, banking and finance, food and water—necessary to sustain modern society and the lives of 310 million Americans.

Passage of the SHIELD Act to protect the National electric grid is urgently necessary. In 2010, after the House unanimously passed the GRID Act, if one Senator had not put a hold on the bill, today in 2014 the Nation would already be protected, since it would take about 3.5 years to harden the grid.

Passage of the Critical Infrastructure Protection Act (CIPA) to create a new National Planning Scenario focused on EMP is urgently necessary. As the National Planning Scenarios are the basis for all Federal, State, and local emergency planning, training, and resource allocation, an EMP National Planning Scenario would immediately and significantly improve National preparedness for an EMP catastrophe.

The single most important thing Congress could do to protect the American people from EMP, and from all other threats to critical infrastructures, is pass the Critical Infrastructure Protection Act, which bill is or soon will be before this committee for consideration.

Thousands of emergency planners and first responders at the Federal, State, and local level want to protect our Nation and their States and communities from the EMP threat. But they are seriously hindered and even prohibited from doing so because the EMP threat is not among the 15 canonical National Planning Scenarios utilized by the Department of Homeland Security.

Passage of the Critical Infrastructure Protection Act would immediately mobilize thousands of emergency planners and first responders at all levels of government, and educate millions of others, about the EMP threat and how to prepare for it.

Passage of the Critical Infrastructure Protection Act would immediately help States that are frustrated with lack of action on EMP in Washington, and are trying to launch initiatives protecting their electrical grids from EMP, as is being attempted now in Maine, Virginia, Oklahoma, and Florida. Passage of the Critical Infrastructure Protection Act would educate all States about the EMP threat and help them protect their critical infrastructures.

For example, projects in New York and Massachusetts to harden their State grids against severe weather caused by climate change should include protection against an EMP event, which is the worst threat to the grid. If the grid is protected against EMP, it will mitigate all lesser threats, including cyber attack, sabotage, and severe weather.

Given the amounts of money being spent in New York and Massachusetts on grid hardening against severe weather, significant EMP protection can probably be accomplished now within their current budgets. But the cost of EMP protection will increase significantly if they delay and attempt remediation later.

EMP is a clear and present danger. A Carrington-class coronal mass ejection narrowly missed the Earth in July 2012. Last April, during the nuclear crisis with North Korea over Kim Jong-Un's threatened nuclear strikes against the United States, Pyongyang apparently practiced an EMP attack with its KSM–3 satellite, that passed over the U.S. heartland and over the Washington, D.C.-New York City corridor. Iran, estimated to be within 2 months of nuclear weapons by the administration, has a demonstrated capability to launch an EMP attack from a vessel at sea. The Iranian Revolutionary Guard Navy commenced patrols off the East Coast of the United States in February.

Thank you for your attention to EMP, which is the least understood but gravest threat to our society. This concludes my remarks.

ATTACHMENT

WHAT IS EMP?

Nuclear, Natural, and Non-Nuclear EMP

An electromagnetic pulse (EMP) is a super-energetic radio wave that can destroy, damage, or cause the malfunction of electronic systems by overloading their circuits. EMP is harmless to people biologically, passing through their bodies without injury, like a radio wave. But by damaging electronic systems that make modern society possible, that enable computers to function and airliners to fly for example, EMP can cause mass destruction of property and life.

A single nuclear weapon detonated at high altitude will generate an electromagnetic pulse that can cause catastrophic damage across the entire contiguous United States to the critical infrastructures—electric power, telecommunications, transportation, banking and finance, food and water—that sustain modern civilization and the lives of 310 million Americans. Nature can also generate an EMP causing similarly catastrophic consequences across the entire contiguous United States— or even across the entire planet—by means of a solar flare from the Sun that causes on Earth a great geomagnetic storm. Non-nuclear weapons, often referred to as radio frequency weapons, can also generate an EMP, much more limited in range than a nuclear weapon, that can damage electronics, and could cause the collapse of critical infrastructures locally, perhaps with cascading effects over an area as large as a major city.

NUCLEAR EMP

Any nuclear warhead detonated at high altitude, 30 kilometers or more above the Earth's surface, will generate an electromagnetic pulse. The immediate effects of EMP are disruption of, and damage to, electronic systems and electrical infrastructure. EMP is not reported in the scientific literature to have direct harmful effects on people. Because an EMP attack would detonate a nuclear warhead at high-altitude, no other nuclear effects—such as blast, thermal radiation, or radioactive fallout—would be experienced by people on the ground or flying through the atmosphere. However, because modern civilization and life itself now depends upon electricity and electronics, an EMP attack is a high-tech means of killing millions of people the old-fashioned way—through starvation, disease, and societal collapse.

Gamma rays, and the fireball from a high-altitude nuclear detonation, interact with the atmosphere to produce a super-energetic radio wave—the EMP—that covers everything within line-of-sight from the explosion to the Earth's horizon. Thus, even a relatively low-altitude EMP attack, where the nuclear warhead is detonated at an altitude of 30 kilometers, will generate a damaging EMP field over a vast area, covering a region equivalent to New England, all of New York, and half of Pennsylvania. A nuclear weapon detonated at an altitude of 400 kilometers over the center of the United States would place an EMP field over the entire contiguous United States and parts of Canada and Mexico.

The EMP generated by a nuclear weapon has three components, designated by the U.S. scientific-technical community E1, E2, and E3.

E1 is caused by gamma rays, emitted by the nuclear warhead, that knocks electrons off of molecules in the upper atmosphere, causing the electrons to rotate rapidly around the lines of the Earth's magnetic field, a phenomenon termed the Compton Effect. The E1 component of nuclear EMP is a shockwave, transmitting thousands of volts of energy in mere nanoseconds of time, and having a high-frequency (short) wavelength that can couple directly into small objects, like personal computers, automobiles, and transformers. E1 is unique to nuclear weapons and is too fast and too energetic to be arrested by protective devices used for lightning.

The E2 component of a nuclear EMP is comparable to lightning in its energetic content and medium (milliseconds) frequency and wavelength. Protective devices used for lightning are effective against E2.

E3 is caused by the fireball of a nuclear explosion, the expanding and then collapsing fireball causing the Earth's magnetic field to oscillate, generating electric currents in the very large objects that can couple into the low frequency, long (seconds) wavelength part of the EMP that is E3. The E3 waveform can couple directly only into objects having at least one dimension of great length. Electric power and telecommunications lines, that run for kilometers in many directions, are ideally suited for receiving E3. Although E3 compared to E1 appears to deliver little energy, just volts per meter, this is multiplied manifold by power and telecommunications lines that are typically many kilometers long, building up E3 currents that can melt Extremely High-Voltage (EHV) transformers, typically designed to handle 750,000 volts. Small electronics can also be destroyed by E3 if they are connected in any way to an E3 receiver—like a personal computer plugged into an electric outlet, which of course is connected to power lines that are ideal E3 receivers, or like the electronic servo-mechanisms that operate the controls of large passenger airliners, that can receive E3 through the metal skin of the aircraft wings and body.

Protective devices used for lightning are not effective against E3, that can build up energy sufficient to overwhelm lightning arrestors and bypass them through electrical arcing.

EMP and its effects were observed during the U.S. and Soviet atmospheric test programs in 1962. The 1962 U.S. STARFISH nuclear detonation—not designed or intended as an EMP generator—at an altitude of about 400 kilometers above Johnston Island in the Pacific Ocean, surprised the U.S. scientific community by producing EMP. Some electronic systems in the Hawaiian Islands, 1,400 kilometers distant, were affected, causing the failure of street lights, tripping circuit breakers, triggering burglar alarms, and damage to telecommunications. In their testing that year, the Soviets executed a series of nuclear detonations in which they exploded 300 kiloton weapons at approximately 300, 150, and 60 kilometers above their test site in South Central Asia. They report that on each shot they observed damage to overhead and underground buried cables at distances of 600 kilometers. They also observed surge arrestor burnout, spark-gap breakdown, blown fuses, and power supply breakdowns.

In the years since 1962, the U.S. scientific and defense community established incontrovertibly, by means of nuclear tests and EMP simulators, that an EMP attack could have catastrophic effects by destroying electronic systems over broad regions—potentially over the entire contiguous United States.

Because so much information about EMP was largely Classified for so long, myths abound about EMP, that the EMP Commission has endeavored to correct in its Unclassified reports and briefings. For example, a high-yield nuclear weapon is not necessary to make an EMP attack. Although a high-yield weapon will generally make a more powerful EMP field than a low-yield nuclear weapon, ALL nuclear weapons produce gamma rays and EMP. The EMP Commission found, by testing modern electronics in simulators, that ANY nuclear weapon can potentially make a catastrophic EMP attack on the United States. Even a very low-yield nuclear weapon—like a 1-kiloton nuclear artillery shell—will produce enough EMP to pose a catastrophic threat. This is so in part because the U.S. electric grid is so aged and overburdened, and because the high-tech electronics that support the electric grid and other critical infrastructures are over 1 million times more vulnerable to EMP than the electronics of the 1960s.

The EMP Commission also found that, contrary to the claim that high-yield nuclear weapons are necessary for an EMP attack, that very low-yield nuclear weapons of special design can produce significantly more EMP than high-yield nuclear weapons. The EMP Commission found further that Russia, probably China, and possibly North Korea are already in possession of such weapons. Russian military writings call these "Super-EMP" nuclear weapons, and credibly claim that they can generate 200 kilovolts per meter—many times the 30 KVs/meter attributed to a high-yield (20 megaton) nuclear weapon of normal design. Yet a Super-EMP warhead can have a tiny explosive yield, perhaps only 1 kiloton, because it is specially designed to produce primarily gamma rays that generate the E1 electromagnetic shockwave component of the EMP effect. Super-EMP weapons are specialized to generate an overwhelming E1, and produce no E2 or E3 but do not need to, as their E1 is so potent.

In 2004, credible Russian sources warned the EMP Commission that design information and "brain drain" from Russia had transferred to North Korea the capability to build a Super-EMP nuclear weapon "within a few years." In 2006 and again in 2008, North Korea tested a nuclear device of very low yield, 1–3 kilotons, and declared these tests successful. South Korean military intelligence, in open-source reporting, independently corroborates the Russian warning that North Korea is developing a Super-EMP nuclear warhead. North Korea's proclivity to sell anything to anyone, including missiles and nuclear technology to fellow rogue nations Iran and Syria, makes Pyongyang's possession of Super-EMP nuclear weapons especially worrisome.

Another myth is that rogue states or terrorists need a sophisticated intercontinental ballistic missile to make an EMP attack. In fact, any missile, including short-range missiles that can deliver a nuclear warhead to an altitude of 30 kilometers or more, can make a catastrophic EMP attack on the United States, by launching off a ship or freighter. Indeed, Iran has practiced ship-launched EMP attacks using Scud missiles—which are in the possession of scores of nations and even terrorist groups. An EMP attack launched off a ship, since Scuds are common-place and a warhead detonated in outer space would leave no bomb debris for forensic analysis, could enable rogue states or terrorists to destroy U.S. critical infrastructures and kill millions of Americans anonymously.

NATURAL EMP

Mother Nature can also pose an EMP threat. The Sun emits solar flares and coronal mass ejections that can strike the Earth's magnetosphere and generate a natural EMP in the form of a geomagnetic storm. Geomagnetic storms rarely affect the United States, but regularly damage nations located at high northern latitudes, such as Canada, Norway, Sweden, Finland, and Russia. Damage from a normal geomagnetic storm can be severe. For example, in 1989 a geomagnetic storm over Canada destroyed the electric power grid in Quebec.

The EMP Commission was the first to discover and report in 2004 that every hundred years or so the Sun produces a great geomagnetic storm. Great geomagnetic storms produce effects similar to the E3 EMP from a multi-megaton nuclear weapon, and so large that it would cover the entire United States—possibly even the entire planet. Geomagnetic storms, even great geomagnetic storms, generate no E1 or E2, only E3, technically called the magnetohydrodynamic EMP.

Nonetheless, E3 alone from a great geomagnetic storm is sufficient to end modern civilization. The EMP produced, given the current state of unpreparedness by the United States and every nation on Earth, could collapse power grids everywhere on the planet and destroy EHV transformers and other electronic systems that would require years to repair or replace.

Modern civilization cannot exist for a protracted period without electricity. Within days of a blackout across the United States, a blackout that could encompass the entire planet, emergency generators would run out of fuel, telecommunications would cease as would transportation due to gridlock, and eventually no fuel. Cities would have no running water and soon, within a few days, exhaust their food supplies. Police, Fire, Emergency Services and hospitals cannot long operate in a blackout. Government and industry also need electricity in order to operate.

The EMP Commission warns that a natural or nuclear EMP event, given current unpreparedness, would likely result in societal collapse.

The last great geomagnetic storm was in 1859, called the "Carrington Event" after the astronomer who noted the phenomenon. The 1859 great geomagnetic storm caused fires in telegraph stations and burned the just-laid transatlantic cable, but its effects were not catastrophic because electronic systems were few and not essential to society in 1859. Great geomagnetic storms are recognizable in historical records because they produce highly unusual effects, like the appearance of the Aurora Borealis at the equator, that even common people often record in letters and diaries. No great geomagnetic storm has occurred in the modern era, in which society depends for its very existence on electronics. Most specialists believe a great geomagnetic storm is overdue, since this once-a-century phenomenon last occurred in 1859. Many scientists believe a great geomagnetic storm is most likely to occur during the solar maximum, when solar flares and coronal mass ejections that cause geomagnetic storms increase sharply in frequency. The solar maximum recurs every 11 years, next in 2012–2013.

NASA and the National Academy of Sciences (NAS) published a blue-ribbon study independently confirming the warning of the EMP Commission about the threat posed by a great geomagnetic storm. The EMP Commission and the NASA–NAS reports, and several subsequent independent studies, conclude that if a great geomagnetic storm like the 1859 Carrington Event happened today, millions could die.

NON-NUCLEAR EMP WEAPONS

Radiofrequency weapons of widely varying designs—some using conventional explosions to generate an EMP, others using microwave emitters to direct energy at a target, for example—can destroy, damage, and disrupt electronic systems at short ranges. Non-nuclear EMP weapons seldom have ranges or a radius of effect greater than 1 kilometer, and usually much less than this.

Some scientists credibly claim that non-nuclear EMP weapons can be developed having a radius of effect of tens of kilometers. However, no nation has yet demonstrated such a capability, including the United States, which has worked to develop advanced radiofrequency weapons for many years. Even such advanced non-nuclear EMP weapons would still be limited and localized in their effects, compared to the Nation-wide effects of a nuclear EMP attack or the planetary effects of a great geomagnetic storm.

Microwave radiation is the lethal mechanism usually employed by non-nuclear EMP weapons, an effect somewhat comparable but not identical to E1 from a nuclear weapon. Radiofrequency weapons produce no E2 or E3 pulse.

Terrorists, criminals, and even lone individuals can build a non-nuclear EMP weapon without great trouble or expense, working from Unclassified designs publicly available on the internet, and using parts available at any electronics store. In 2000, the Terrorism Panel of the House Armed Services Committee sponsored an experiment, recruiting a small team of amateur electronics enthusiasts to attempt constructing a radiofrequency weapon, relying only on Unclassified design information and parts purchased from Radio Shack. The team, in 1 year, built two radiofrequency weapons of radically different designs. One was designed to fit inside the shipping crate for a Xerox machine, so it could be delivered to the Pentagon mail room where (in those more unguarded days before 9/11) it could slowly fry the Pentagon's computers. The other radiofrequency weapon was designed to fit inside a small Volkswagon bus, so it could be driven down Wall Street and disrupt computers—and perhaps the National economy.

Both designs were demonstrated and tested successfully during a special Congressional hearing for this purpose at the U.S. Army's Aberdeen Proving Ground.

Radiofrequency weapons are not merely a hypothetical threat. Terrorists, criminals, and disgruntled individuals have used home-made radiofrequency weapons. The U.S. military and foreign militaries have a wide variety of such weaponry.

Moreover, non-nuclear EMP devices that could be used as radiofrequency weapons are publicly marketed for sale to anyone, usually advertised as "EMP simulators." For example, one such simulator is advertised for public sale as an "EMP Suitcase." This EMP simulator is designed to look like a suitcase, can be carried and operated by one person, and is purpose-built with a high energy radiofrequency output to destroy electronics. However, it has only a short radius of effect. Nonetheless, a terrorist or deranged individual who knows what he is doing, who has studied the electric grid for a major metropolitan area, could—armed with the "EMP Suitcase"—black out a major city.

A CLEAR AND PRESENT DANGER

Emphasis is warranted that the nuclear EMP threat is not merely theoretical—it is real, a clear and present danger. Nuclear EMP attack is the perfect asymmetric weapon for state actors who wish to level the battlefield by neutralizing the great technological advantage enjoyed by U.S. military forces. EMP is also the ideal means, the only means, whereby rogue states or terrorists could use a single nuclear weapon to destroy the United States and prevail in the War on Terrorism or some other conflict with a single blow. The EMP Commission also warned that states or terrorists could exploit U.S. vulnerability to EMP attack for coercion or blackmail: "Therefore, terrorists or state actors that possess relatively unsophisticated missiles armed with nuclear weapons may well calculate that, instead of destroying a city or military base, they may obtain the greatest political-military utility from one or a few such weapons by using them—or threatening their use—in an EMP attack."

The EMP Commission found that states such as Russia, China, North Korea, and Iran have incorporated EMP attack into their military doctrines, and openly describe making EMP attacks against the United States. Indeed, the EMP Commission was established by Congress partly in response to a Russian nuclear EMP threat made to an official Congressional Delegation on May 2, 1999, in the midst of the Balkans crisis. Vladimir Lukin, head of the Russian delegation and a former Ambassador to the United States, warned: "Hypothetically, if Russia really wanted to hurt the United States in retaliation for NATO's bombing of Yugoslavia, Russia could fire an SLBM and detonate a single nuclear warhead at high altitude over the United States. The resulting EMP would massively disrupt U.S. communications and computer systems, shutting down everything."

China's military doctrine also openly describes EMP attack as the ultimate asymmetric weapon, as it strikes at the very technology that is the basis of U.S. power. Where EMP is concerned, "The United States is more vulnerable to attacks than any other country in the world":

"Some people might think that things similar to the 'Pearl Harbor Incident' are unlikely to take place during the information age. Yet it could be regarded as the 'Pearl Harbor Incident' of the 21st Century if a surprise attack is conducted against the enemy's crucial information systems of command, control, and communications by such means as . . . electromagnetic pulse weapons . . . Even a superpower like the United States, which possesses nuclear missiles and powerful armed forces, cannot guarantee its immunity . . . In their own words, a highly computerized open society like the United States is extremely vulnerable to electronic attacks from all sides. This is because the U.S. economy, from banks to telephone systems and from power plants to iron and steel works, relies entirely on computer networks . . . When a country grows increasingly powerful economically and technologically . . . it will become increasingly dependent on modern information systems . . . The United States is more vulnerable to attacks than any other country in the world."

Iran—the world's leading sponsor of international terrorism—in military writings openly describes EMP as a terrorist weapon, and as the ultimate weapon for prevailing over the West: "If the world's industrial countries fail to devise effective ways to defend themselves against dangerous electronic assaults, then they will disintegrate within a few years . . . American soldiers would not be able to find food to eat nor would they be able to fire a single shot."

The threats are not merely words. The EMP Commission assesses that Russia has, as it openly declares in military writings, probably developed what Russia describes as a "Super-EMP" nuclear weapon—specifically designed to generate extraordinarily high EMP fields in order to paralyze even the best protected U.S. strategic and military forces. China probably also has Super-EMP weapons. North Korea too may possess or be developing a Super-EMP nuclear weapon, as alleged by credible Russian sources to the EMP Commission, and by open-source reporting from South Korean military intelligence. But any nuclear weapon, even a low-yield first generation device, could suffice to make a catastrophic EMP attack on the United States. Iran, although it is assessed as not yet having the bomb, is actively testing missile delivery systems and has practiced launches of its best missile, the Shahab–III, fuzing for high-altitude detonations, in exercises that look suspiciously like training for making EMP attacks. As noted earlier, Iran has also practiced launching from a ship a Scud, the world's most common missile—possessed by over 60 nations, terrorist groups, and private collectors. A Scud might be the ideal choice for a ship-launched EMP attack against the United States intended to be executed anonymously, to escape any last-gasp U.S. retaliation. Unlike a nuclear weapon detonated in a city, a high-altitude EMP attack leaves no bomb debris for forensic analysis, no perpetrator "fingerprints."

EMP VULNERABILITIES

Today's microelectronics are the foundation of our modern civilization, but are over 1 million times more vulnerable to EMP than the far more primitive and robust electronics of the 1960s, that proved vulnerable during nuclear EMP tests of that era. Tests conducted by the EMP Commission confirmed empirically the theory that, as modern microelectronics become ever smaller and more efficient, and operate ever faster on lower voltages, they also become ever more vulnerable, and can be destroyed or disrupted by much lower EMP field strengths.

Microelectronics and electronic systems are everywhere, and run virtually everything in the modern world. All of the civilian critical infrastructures that sustain the economy of the United States, and the lives of 310 million Americans, depend, directly or indirectly, upon electricity and electronic systems.

Of special concern is the vulnerability to EMP of the Extra-High-Voltage (EHV) transformers, that are indispensable to the operation of the electric grid. EHV transformers drive electric current over long distances, from the point of generation to consumers (from the Niagara Falls hydroelectric facility to New York City, for example). The electric grid cannot operate without EHV transformers—which could be destroyed by an EMP event. The United States no longer manufactures EHV transformers. They must be manufactured and imported from overseas, from Germany or South Korea, the only two nations in the world that manufacture such transformers for export. Each EHV transformer must be custom-made for its unique role in the grid. A single EHV transformer typically requires 18 months to manufacture. The loss of large numbers of EHV transformers to an EMP event would plunge the United States into a protracted blackout lasting years, with perhaps no hope of eventual recovery, as the society and population probably could not survive for even 1 year without electricity.

Another key vulnerability to EMP are Supervisory Control And Data Acquisition systems (SCADAs). SCADAs essentially are small computers, numbering in the millions and ubiquitous everywhere in the critical infrastructures, that perform jobs previously performed by hundreds of thousands of human technicians during the 1960s and before, in the era prior to the microelectronics revolution. SCADAs do things like regulating the flow of electricity into a transformer, controlling the flow of gas through a pipeline, or running traffic control lights. SCADAs enable a few dozen people to run the critical infrastructures for an entire city, whereas previously hundreds or even thousands of technicians were necessary. Unfortunately, SCADAs are especially vulnerable to EMP.

EHV transformers and SCADAs are the most important vulnerabilities to EMP, but are by no means the only vulnerabilities. Each of the critical infrastructures has their own unique vulnerabilities to EMP:

The National electric grid, with its transformers and generators and electronic controls and thousands of miles of power lines, is a vast electronic machine—more vulnerable to EMP than any other critical infrastructure. Yet the electric grid is the most important of all critical infrastructures, and is in fact the keystone supporting modern civilization, as it powers all the other critical infrastructures. As of now it is our technological Achilles Heel. The EMP Commission found that, if the electric grid collapses, so too will collapse all the other critical infrastructures. But, if the electric grid can be protected and recovered, so too all the other critical infrastructures can also be restored.

Transportation is a critical infrastructure because modern civilization cannot exist without the goods and services moved by road, rail, ship, and air. Cars, trucks, locomotives, ships, and aircraft all have electronic components, motors, and controls that are potentially vulnerable to EMP. Traffic control systems that avert traffic jams and collisions for road, rail, and air depend upon electronic systems, that the EMP Commission discovered are especially vulnerable to EMP. Gas stations, fuel pipelines, and refineries that make petroleum products depend upon electronic components and cannot operate without electricity. Given our current state of unpreparedness, in the aftermath of a natural or nuclear EMP event, transportation systems would be paralyzed.

Communications is a critical infrastructure because modern economies and the cohesion and operation of modern societies depend to a degree unprecedented in history on the rapid movement of information—accomplished today mostly by electronic means. Telephones, cell phones, personal computers, television, and radio are all directly vulnerable to EMP, and cannot operate without electricity. Satellites that operate at Low-Earth-Orbit (LEO) for communications, weather, scientific, and military purposes are vulnerable to EMP and to collateral effects from an EMP attack. Within weeks of an EMP event, the LEO satellites, which comprise most satellites, would probably be inoperable. In the aftermath of a nuclear or natural EMP event, under present levels of preparedness, communications would be severely limited, restricted mainly to those few military communications networks that are hardened against EMP.

Banking and finance are the critical infrastructure that sustain modern economies. Whether it is the stock market, the financial records of a multinational corporation, or the ATM card of an individual—financial transactions and record keeping all depend now at the macro- and micro-level upon computers and electronic automated systems. Many of these are directly vulnerable to EMP, and none can operate without electricity. The EMP Commission found that an EMP event could transform the modern electronic economy into a feudal economy based on barter.

Food has always been vital to every person and every civilization. The critical infrastructure for producing, delivering, and storing food depends upon a complex web of technology, including machines for planting and harvesting and packaging, refrigerated vehicles for long-haul transportation, and temperature-controlled warehouses. Modern technology enables over 98 percent of the U.S. National population to be fed by less than 2 percent of the population. Huge regional warehouses that resupply supermarkets constitute the National food reserves, enough food to feed the Nation for 30–60 days at normal consumption rates, the warehoused food preserved by refrigeration and temperature control systems that typically have enough emergency electrical power (diesel or gas generators) to last only about an average of 3 days. Experience with storm-induced blackouts proves that when these big regional food warehouses lose electrical power, most of the food supply will rapidly spoil. Farmers, less than 2 percent of the population as noted above, cannot feed 310 million Americans if deprived of the means that currently makes possible this technological miracle.

Water too has always been a basic necessity to every person and civilization, even more crucial than food. The critical infrastructure for purifying and delivering potable water, and for disposing of and treating waste water, is a vast networked machine powered by electricity that uses electrical pumps, screens, filters, paddles, and sprayers to purify and deliver drinkable water, and to remove and treat waste water. Much of the machinery in the water infrastructure is directly vulnerable to EMP. The system cannot operate without vast amounts of electricity supplied by the power grid. A natural or nuclear EMP event would immediately deprive most of the U.S. National population of running water. Many natural sources of water—lakes, streams, and rivers—would be dangerously polluted by toxic wastes from sewage, industry, and hospitals that would backflow from or bypass wastewater treatment plants, that could no longer intake and treat pollutants without electric power. Many natural water sources that would normally be safe to drink, after an EMP event, would be polluted with human wastes including feces, industrial wastes including arsenic and heavy metals, and hospital wastes including pathogens.

Emergency services such as police, fire, and hospitals are the critical infrastructure that upholds the most basic functions of government and society—preserving law and order, protecting property and life. Experience from protracted storm-induced blackouts has shown, for example in the aftermath of Hurricanes Andrew and Katrina, that when the lights go out and communications systems fail and there is no gas for squad cars, fire trucks, and ambulances, the worst elements of society and the worst human instincts rapidly takeover. The EMP Commission found that, given our current state of unpreparedness, a natural or nuclear EMP event could create anarchic conditions that would profoundly challenge the existence of social order.

Mr. PERRY. Thank you, Dr. Pry.

The Chairman now recognizes Dr. Frankel for 5 minutes.

STATEMENT OF MICHAEL J. FRANKEL, SENIOR SCIENTIST, PENN STATE UNIVERSITY, APPLIED RESEARCH LABORATORY

Mr. FRANKEL. Thank you, Mr. Chairman, honorable Members. My name is Mike Frankel. As the initial bio mentioned, I am a theoretical physicist by trade. I have spent much of my career in Government service with a focus on understanding nuclear weapons and their effects. I am appearing before you today pursuant to my service as the executive director of the EMP Commission during the entire span of its activity. I have provided extended remarks for the record, and what I wish to do in the few moments here is just make a few summary remarks and recommendations.

There are a number of important legacies of the Commission; not the least, as Dr. Pry just mentioned, is highlighting the effects of a so-called supersolar storm, which was first identified as a vulnerability by the Commission and I think is now part of the regular discourse, and which the Nation is still, as far as I can see, unprepared to deal with.

Another important analytic insight provided by the Commission was its understanding and raising the alarm for the prospect of simultaneous failures of the system. All engineers design their systems against single-point failure. We saw an instance of that. Recently there was an incident reported in the Wall Street Journal where a PG&E substation was attacked by an individual, individuals with rifles. The entire substation went off-line. Transformers were damaged, but the population didn't notice anything. It was a single-point failure of a single station. The control systems functioned as they were supposed to. Electricity was rerouted, et cetera.

It was the large number of failures that the EMP Commission analyzed that fall within a large geographical area provided by the EMP footprint which kind-of raised the alarm of many multiple failures. Nobody designs against multiple failures. Here and there you may find some engineers who design against two simultaneous failures. But these failures can be affected not just by EMP. They could be affected by cyber. The important thing is that if there are simultaneous failures over large areas, the analysis of the Commission was things are very likely to fail, and restoration will take a very long time.

Another important point which I would like to make here, which wasn't made by the EMP Commission in its report, is the nexus between EMP and cyber. Both of those are modes of attack on our electronic systems which sustain our society. They work even kind-of in the same way. They reach out through the electrical distribution system, and they inflict currents, voltages on the system so the system will not operate the way the owner expects them to. If resources are being allocated to prevent the cyber threat, it seems foolish not to also address at the same time one end of the cyber threat, which is the EMP, kind-of the "stupid cyber", if you will.

Finally, what I would like to do in the last minute or so that I have left is touch on the reception which the EMP Commission's recommendations received. The recommendations were pointed towards both the Defense Department and to the Department of Homeland Security. The Secretary of Defense considered the recommendations; in fact, concurred with most of them. An action plan was promulgated. Funds were allocated in the outyears. The Defense Science Board was stood up, and essentially EMP research and alertness was reinvigorated within the Department of Defense and the acquisition community there.

No similar reaction was noted in the Department of Homeland Security. There was no office of responsibility designated at a confirmed level. Funds weren't POM'd. There are still 75 recommendations pointed towards the Department of Homeland Security within its purview that could increase the resilience, survivability, and recovery of our electric grid were it subject to such an event, and it will be, at least through the natural EMP of the sun; and something needs doing, and now is the time to do it.

I thank you for the opportunity to make these remarks, and that concludes my own remarks. Thank you.

[The prepared statement of Mr. Frankel follows:]

PREPARED STATEMENT OF MICHAEL J. FRANKEL

MAY 8, 2014

Mr. Chairman and Honorable Members of the committee, thank you for the opportunity to testify today about an important but relatively neglected vulnerability that affects the resilience of all of our Nation's critical infrastructures. My name is Mike Frankel. I'm a theoretical physicist by trade and presently a member of the senior scientific staff at Penn State University's Applied Research Laboratory. I've spent a career in Government service developing technical and scientific expertise on the effects of nuclear weapons, managing WMD programs, and performing scientific research in a variety of National security positions with the Navy, the old Defense Nuclear Agency, and the Office of the Secretary of Defense. I appear before you today pursuant my service as the executive director of the EMP Commission during its entire span of activity, commencing with authorization if the Floyd D. Spence National Defense Authorization Act of 2001 and culminating with delivery of its final, Classified, assessment to the Congress in 2009 The conclusions of the Commission were documented in a series of five volumes, three of them Classified, and in particular the Commission's perspectives related to infrastructure protection were documented in an Unclassified volume "Critical National Infrastructures," released in November 2008. What I'd like to do is expand on some of the Commission's conclusions in light of recent developments since submitting our final report. I should also like to emphasize a new topic that was not referenced in that final report, and that is the nexus between the cybersecurity threat and EMP.

One of the major insights of the EMP Commission was to highlight the unique danger to the electric grid caused by simultaneous failures induced by the large number of components that fall within an EMP's damaging footprint on the ground. As first reported in the journal *Foreign Affairs* and picked up a month later by the *Wall Street Journal,* on the night of April 16, 2013, a locked PG&E substation was infiltrated and a number of high-voltage transformers attacked by still-unidentified individuals firing rifles. Damaged transformers went off-line but the SCADA controls automatically re-routed the electrical distribution along alternate paths. In this case, standard engineering practice which designs around the possibility of single point failure, kicked in just as it should, and little effect was noticed by the general population. However, it took nearly a full month to repair the damaged transformers and return them to service. An important analytic contribution of the Commission was to highlight the possibility of highly multiple numbers of component failures, as might be expected within the wide area encompassed by an EMP event footprint. No one designed against such a possibility and it was the Commission's conclusion, based on its own analyses and on a close collaboration with power industry engineers, that such a scenario would inevitably lead to very wide-spread, and very long-term collapse of the Nation's electric grid, with potentially devastating economic and ultimately physical and health consequences. The PG&E incident should remind us that the Commission's analytic insight extends far beyond EMP. While in this case only a single substation was attacked, had there been a coordinated physical attack against many simultaneous targets, or for that matter by localized EMP sources such as readily available HPM/RF sources, it seems inevitable that electric service to much larger fraction of the population would have been compromised and for an indefinitely prolonged period. And of course, the same result could be achieved by simultaneous cyber-attack, with much reduced physical exposure by the perpetrators. So there's a real vulnerability there that needs to be addressed.

I should also like to turn some attention to the generally unremarked overlap between electromagnetic vulnerability of the type described by the EMP Commission and the more general issue of cyber vulnerability. While not often considered in tandem, it is more correct to consider EMP vulnerabilities as one end of a continuous spectrum of cyber threats to our electronic-based infrastructures. They share both an overlap in the effects produced—the failure of electronic systems to perform their function and possibly incurring actual physical damage—as well as their mode of inflicting damage. They both reach out through the connecting electronic distribution systems, and impress unwanted voltages and currents on the connecting wires. In the usual cyber case, those unwanted currents contain information—usually in the form of malicious code—that instructs the system to perform actions unwanted and unanticipated by its owner. In the EMP case, the impressed signal does not contain coded information. It is merely a dump of random noise which may flip bit states, or damage components, and also ensures the system will not behave in the way the owner expects. This electronic noise dump may thus be thought of as a "stupid cyber". When addressing the vulnerability of our infrastructures to the cyber threat, it is important that we not neglect the EMP end of the cyber threat spectrum. And there is another important overlap with the cyber threat. With the grid on the cusp of technological change in the evolution to the "smart grid", the proliferation of sensors and controls which will manage the new grid architecture must be protected against cyber at the same time they must be protected against EMP. Cyber and EMP threats have the unique capability to precipitate highly multiple failures of these many new control systems over a widely distributed geographical area, and such simultaneous failures, as previously discussed, are likely to signal a wider and more long-lasting catastrophe.

Another important legacy of the EMP Commission was to first highlight the danger to our electric grid due to solar storms, which may impress large—and effectively DC—currents on the long runs of conducting cable that make up the distribution system. While this phenomenon has long been known, and protected against, by engineering practices in the power industry, the extreme 100-year storm first analyzed by the Commission is now widely recognized to represent a major danger to our National electrical system for which adequate protective measures have not been taken and whose consequences—the likely collapse of much of the National grid, possibly for a greatly extended period, may rightly be termed catastrophic. At this point, the only scientific controversy attending the likelihood of our system being subject to a so-called super solar storm, is related to the time-constant. But these events have already occurred within the last century or so, they will occur again. We should be ready.

The most important legacy of the EMP Commission however, was in the recommendations which were provided that would, if acted upon, protect key assets of both the civilian and military infrastructures, and it is here that I should like to point to an important divergence in the Government's response. The (Classified) recommendations that were provided to the Department of Defense were formally considered, in the large main concurred with, and then acted upon. The Secretary of Defense issued a Classified action plan, out-year funding was POM'd in the FYDP, an office and an official of responsibility were appointed, a standing Defense Science Board committee was stood up, an active research program is maintained, and survivability and certification instructions were issued by both DOD and by USSTRATCOM. Today, while vigilant oversight continues to be warranted, an EMP awareness pervades our acquisition system and operational doctrine. The response on the civilian side of the equation was not so rosy. The final report of EMP Commission contained 75 recommendations to improve the survivability, operability, resilience, and recovery of all the critical infrastructures, and in particular of the most key of all, the electrical grid. Most of these recommendations were pointed towards the Department of Homeland Security. While there have been some conversations, it has been hard to detect much of an active resonance at all issuing from the Department. They have not, as far as I know, even designated EMP as a one of their 10 of 15 disaster scenarios for advanced planning circumstances. And this at a time when they do include a low-altitude nuclear disaster—certainly disastrous but not one that would produce wide-ranging EMP.

In the end, it is hard to deal with 75 recommendations, all at once. But the solution is not to ignore all of them. If there is only a single essentially a no-cost step I would leave this committee with, it would be to task the Department of Homeland Security with responding to the still-languishing recommendations of the EMP Commission. The Department of Defense did issue a response, as mandated by the legislation which originally created that Commission. But no such mandatory response was levied at the time on the Department of Homeland Security, which did not even exist when the Commission legislation was passed as part of the National Defense Authorization Act of 2001. The DHS should be required to explain which recommendations they concur with and/or with which they non-concur, and why. They should be asked to prioritize amongst the 75 and come back with implementation recommendations, or explain why they think it is unnecessary. And finally, I would also urge the committee to support passage of the Critical Infrastructure Protection Act.

I wish to thank the committee for this opportunity to present my views of this most important issue.

Mr. PERRY. Thank you, Dr. Frankel.

The Chairman will now recognize Dr. Beck for his testimony.

STATEMENT OF CHRIS BECK, VICE PRESIDENT, POLICY AND STRATEGIC INITIATIVES, THE ELECTRIC INFRASTRUCTURE SECURITY COUNCIL

Mr. BECK. Thank you, very much, Chairman Perry, Ranking Member Clarke, Mr. Franks, and Mr. Vela. Thank you for holding this hearing on one of the most significant threats to our National and homeland security.

As was mentioned earlier, before I joined EIS Council, I did work for this committee focusing on critical infrastructure protection and science and technology issues, and it was through that exposure to this particular threat that I found it to be so significant that I wanted to work on it full time.

The Electric Infrastructure Security Council's mission is to work in partnership with Government and corporate stakeholders to host National and international education, planning, and communication initiatives to help improve infrastructure protection against electromagnetic threats, or E-threats, and other hazards. The summary of my remarks basically are gleaned from international summit meetings that EIS Council hosts, and which are chaired by Mr. Franks and Ms. Clarke, and with that, I want to give a summary of some of the findings of those discussions as well as other discussions.

The problem with EMP or GMD is that developed nations are vulnerable to serious National power grid disruption from electromagnetic threats, both natural and malicious. The severity can range from regional blackout with serious economic consequences to, in the worst-case scenario, a catastrophe that would threaten societal continuity.

The timing of the events for severe space weather—the most recent severe events occurred roughly 90 and 150 years ago, but the timing of the next such occurrence, as with all extreme natural disasters, is unknown. Local, or nonnuclear, or subcontinental, or nuclear EMP could also occur at any time, possibly encouraged by ongoing vulnerability or triggered by changing geopolitical realities.

Key questions that need to be addressed are: What should our National strategy be? We could take a couple of approaches there: Hope for the best and accept the status quo; or encourage cost-effective resilience, restoration, and response planning. Looking at response, it is important to define the path, who should be involved, and how broad our response should be.

A common theme of all the many summit deliberations, Government reports, et cetera, over the past several years is that the risks associated with severe E-threats are serious. It is hard to find anyone who would assert that in today's world hoping for the best is a good strategy for GMD, EMP, or intentional electromagnetic interference, or IEMI.

The path forward consists of organization and coordination. Given the grid's organic design, the consensus of Government studies is that a coordinated planning and standards will be important. Finding the best possible balance between broadly-accepted proactive corporate coordination and Government action will be important to assure fast, effective progress in achieving an E-threat-resilient grid.

Who should be involved? Given the likelihood of a large regional power outage after a National or malicious e-threat, power companies will need to be operating in an environment of extensive response and recovery support from Federal and State government authorities, as well as community response, nongovernmental organizations. So the evolution of planning to address these concerns should include the broadest possible involvement of all of these stakeholders, each contributing in its own domain of authority and expertise.

For all E-threats under consideration here, efforts of prevention, if they are to be effective, must primarily be focused where the impact will occur, in the power grid. For severe space weather, there is clearly no other alternative. For malicious threats, EMP and IEMI, U.S. and allied government security officials and experts at the highest level agree that neither deterrence nor active military measures can alone guarantee the security of our homeland against a determined aggressor prepared to use such weapons.

In conclusion, I should note that there appear to be no significant technical or financial barriers to mitigating this threat. The technologies and operational procedures needed are well understood, and the cost, based on both Government estimates and recent corporate experience, is reasonable.

I would welcome the opportunity to discuss any of these points in greater detail, and this concludes my prepared testimony, and I would be happy to answer any questions.

[The prepared statement of Mr. Beck follows:]

PREPARED STATEMENT OF CHRIS BECK

MAY 8, 2014

INTRODUCTION

Good afternoon Chairman Meehan, Ranking Member Clarke, and Members of the subcommittee. Thank you for holding this hearing on one of the most significant threats to our National and Homeland Security. As many of you know, before I joined EIS Council, I worked for this committee, focusing on Critical Infrastructure Protection and Science and Technology issues. It was through that work that I first became aware of the threats facing our critical electric infrastructures, and I found the issue to be so important that I felt compelled to focus on it exclusively.

The Electric Infrastructure Security Council's mission is to work in partnership with Government and corporate stakeholders to host National and international education, planning, and communication initiatives to help improve infrastructure protection against electromagnetic threats (e-threats) and other hazards. E-threats include naturally occurring geomagnetic disturbances (GMD), high-altitude electromagnetic pulses (HEMP) from nuclear weapons, and non-nuclear EMP from intentional electromagnetic interference (IEMI) devices—the focus of today's hearing.

EMP—DEFINING THE ISSUE

The Problem.—Developed nations are vulnerable to serious national power grid disruption from e-threats, both natural and malicious.

The Severity.—The impact can range from a broad regional blackout with serious economic consequences to, in the worst case, a catastrophe that would threaten societal continuity. With even the most benign scenarios projecting high societal costs, the committee is correct to focus on this as an issue deserving serious attention.

The Timing.—For severe space weather, the most recent events occurred roughly 90 and 150 years ago, but the timing of the next such occurrence, as with all extreme natural disasters, is unknown. Either local (non-nuclear) or sub-continental (nuclear) EMP could occur at any time, encouraged by on-going vulnerability, and triggered by changing geopolitical realities.

KEY QUESTIONS

1. What Should Our National Strategy Be?

At top level, there are two alternative paths:
   a. Hope for the best: Accept the status quo.
      i. For severe space weather, this means hoping the most optimistic projections will turn out to be correct, and the impact will not be catastrophic.
      ii. EMP has been called, "The most powerful asymmetric weapon in history." This approach means hoping no terrorist organization or rogue state will ever take advantage of the power of such devastating weapons.
   b. The other alternative:
      Encourage cost-effective resilience, restoration, and response planning.

2. If We Respond, What Is the Path?

How should we address interconnect-wide interdependence, and how should we proceed with implementation?

3. If We Respond, Who Should Be Involved?

Who should take responsibility to define the path, and implement it? How should the balance between public mandates and private, corporate initiative be determined?

4. How Broad Should Our Response Be?

Should both GMD and EMP be included?

CONSENSUS RECOMMENDATIONS

1. Hope vs. Preparation: Choosing a Strategy

A common theme of all the many Government reports studying these risks, also reflected in the deliberations of the Electric Infrastructure Security Summits over the last several years, is that the risks associated with severe e-threats are serious. It is hard to find anyone who would assert that, in today's world, "hoping for the best" is a good strategy for GMD, EMP, or IEMI.

2. What Is the Path?

Our National power grid is organic in design, but administratively complex. This means approaches are needed that address both of these factors.
   • *Organization and coordination.*—Given the grid's organic design, the consensus of Government studies is that coordinated planning and standards will be important. Finding the best possible balance between broadly-accepted, pro-active corporate coordination and Government action will be important to assure fast, effective progress in achieving an e-threat resilient grid.
   • *Technical.*—A key point, not always recognized, is there is no need to "gold plate" the system.
      For Severe Space Weather, there is already growing discussion of a range of strategies, and none of the approaches under active discussion—from planning measures to comprehensive automated hardware protection—appear high in cost, relative to existing logistics budgets and investment models.
      For EMP, protection planning can focus—not on hardening every component in the power grid—but on protection of a fraction of grid facilities and hardware. In other words, enough resilience investment, and associated restoration planning, to protect enough generation resources and critical loads to allow for both effective restoration and for prioritized support to critical users and installations.

2. Who Should Be Involved?

Given the likelihood of a large regional power outage after a natural or malicious e-threat, power companies will need to be operating in an environment of extensive response and recovery support from Federal and State government authorities, as well as community-response NGOs. Thus, the evolution of planning to address these concerns should include the broadest possible involvement of all of these stakeholders, each contributing in its own domain of authority and expertise.

3. How Broad Should Our Scope Be?

For all the E-threats under consideration here, efforts at protection, if they are to be effective, must primarily be focused where the impact will occur—in the power grid. For severe space weather, there is clearly no other alternative. For malicious threats, EMP and IEMI, U.S. and allied government security officials and experts at the highest levels agree that neither deterrence nor active military measures can alone guarantee the security of our homeland against a determined aggressor prepared to use such weapons.

In conclusion, I should note that there appear to be no significant technical or financial barriers to mitigating this threat. The technologies and operational procedures needed are well understood, and the cost—based on both Government estimates and recent corporate experience—is reasonable. One of the primary needs is for education to increase awareness and therefore willingness to address the problem, and for coordination to address the administrative complexity of our Nation's power grid.

This summary of consensus-based themes and recommendations reflects, I believe, not only the conclusions of the many major Government studies of these issues, but also the deliberations of the past four international Electric Infrastructure Security Summits, with participation by the highest levels of many departments and agencies of the U.S. and allied governments, and of a broad range of scientists and domain experts working in this field.

I would welcome the opportunity to discuss any of these points in greater detail.

This concludes my prepared testimony, and I would be happy to answer any questions.

Mr. PERRY. Thank you, Dr. Beck.

The Chairman now recognizes himself for 5 minutes for questions. These generally go out to each one of you, and one just came to mind as Dr. Beck was talking.

So let me ask you this. If we do harden and protect the grid, but this affects potentially all electric and electronic devices, so even though we harden the grid and power stations and can produce power and so on and so forth, will the systems in individual homes and businesses, like refrigerators and heating and cooling systems, will they be affected to the point where they will all need to be replaced, or even while we have power to our homes, none of the lights will come on and so on so forth? Can anybody illuminate the answer to that question?

Mr. PRY. Well, it depends on the scenario. If you are talking about a geomagnetic storm, it puts at the wavelength of that, which we call E3, or magnetohydrodynamic EMP is so long that it needs to couple into long lines, like power lines, railroad tracks. It won't couple into automobiles, refrigerators, personal computers, and things of that sort. So under that scenario, yes, if you basically keep the electric grid on, you will be able to recover the rest of the society pretty promptly.

In the nuclear case of a nuclear EMP, it has an electromagnetic shock wave that we call E1. This can couple into personal computers, automobiles, and the like, and so you will have deeper societal damage; but then, again, it depends on the kind of weapon used. If it is a primitive, first-generation nuclear weapon, you know, it is not likely to do that across the whole country. It would be more limited to a several-State-size region. If it is the worst-case kind of a nuclear weapon, like a super EMP weapon, which is what we think Russia, China, and probably North Korea have, you know, then you are talking about a scenario where you are having massive, deep damage to personal computers, and refrigerators, and lights and the rest. But if you don't have the bulk power system surviving, there is no hope of recovery under those circumstances. Under that worst-case scenario, what you are doing is you are mitigating a catastrophe and turning it into a manageable disaster, a situation where you won't have massive loss of life, hopefully.

Mr. PERRY. Next question I have is we know that the EPA has promulgated a bevy of regulations on power plants under the current administration. Probably the most obtrusive regulation has been the Mercury and Air Toxics rule, or utility MACT, which has shut down numerous power plants across the country, and there is a claim that some power plants are grandfathered in and avoid updating their facilities in order to avoid new regulations from the EPA.

Do you have any knowledge, is it possible that some power plants are unwilling to update their facilities and protect against EMP attacks in order to avoid new regulations from the EPA? Is there any knowledge here based to answer that question? It might not necessarily be for you folks here, but——

Mr. FRANKEL. I have no specific knowledge about that, but I do know that the power companies are generally reluctant go in and try to refit the generation plants. Any time you ask people to spend money and that it sounds like a mandate to them, there is a reflexive negativity to that.

Mr. PERRY. Sure.

How would you rate the likelihood that the United States will face an EMP event from either a high-altitude electromagnetic pulse, a HEMP, or a massive solar storm?

Mr. FRANKEL. I will take that one. You guys can as well.

I think that the likelihood that the United States will face at some point a so-called massive solar storm, and thus our entire system will be under the footprint, if you will, of a massive solar storm, is about 100 percent. It will happen. The uncertainty here, I believe, is the time constant. It could happen next year, it could be 100 years, but probably not 1,000 years.

The probability that we will be faced with a nuclear HEMP I would say is unknown. I don't call it high. I don't call it low. I would say it is an unknown probability.

Mr. BECK. I would agree with both of those statements.

Mr. PRY. I would concur and also point out that the National Intelligence Council that writes the Classified National intelligence estimates and speaks for the whole U.S. intelligence community considered this issue so important that they put out an Unclassified study called Global Trends 2030, which is available on the internet, that describes eight black swan scenarios that could alter the course of global civilization by or before 2030. In the judgment of the National Intelligence Council, the recurrence of something like a Carrington Event, a geomagnetic superstorm, is one of those events that by or before 2030 could change the course of global civilization.

Mr. PERRY. That is hardly comforting.

My time, however, has expired, so the Chairman recognizes the Ranking Member of the subcommittee, Ms. Clarke, for questions.

Ms. CLARKE. I thank you, Mr. Chairman, and I thank our witnesses for their testimony here today.

I just wanted to clarify for the record from Dr. Pry and Dr. Frankel, I see that both of you served as staff on the EMP Commission in 2004 or thereabouts, but I am trying to get a sense of what organizations you are representing today, and how can we learn more about those organizations?

Mr. FRANKEL. I am representing only my status as a senior scientist at the Penn State University. I am not representing—I do some work for the Department of Defense, but I am in no way representing them.

Ms. CLARKE. You are not representing Penn State either, are you?

Mr. FRANKEL. No. Penn State, I would say, does not have a position about EMP.

Mr. PRY. We both served on the Congressional EMP Commission through its life, from 2001 to 2008. I am currently the executive director of the Task Force on National and Homeland Security, which was an effort to continue the EMP Commission, because the Commissioners, including the chairman, believed it was terminated prematurely before its work was completed. So this task force is an attempt to continue the EMP Commission in some way. Dr. Graham, for example, who is the chairman of that Commission, is the chairman of my task force, and I am here today representing the task force.

Ms. CLARKE. Okay. Very well. Thank you very much.

First of all, I wanted to ask, Mr. Chairman, if we could submit for the record the international E-Pro report. This report was prepared by Dr. Beck under a DOE contract and describes EMP status internationally.

Mr. PERRY. Without objection, so ordered.*

Ms. CLARKE. For our colleagues, there are additional copies on the table for those who may be interested.

Dr. Beck, we all know that extreme atmospheric weather and solar weather that could potentially produce EMPs and other natural disasters can threaten lives, disable communities, and devastate generation transmission and distribution systems. Efforts to harden the electricity grid must focus on three elements: Prevention, recovery, and survivability, and these elements will apply to a situation in which a potential EMP event is involved.

A recent storm such as Hurricane Sandy, which affected my district, pinpointing affected areas was problematic as was finding a clear route for crews through streets that were blocked by fallen trees. As a result, crews were sometimes idled because they could not reach affected areas.

First, preventing this kind of damage in the distribution system will require changes in design standards and construction guidelines, maintenance routines, and inspection procedures. Second, recovery and resiliency planning ought to provide for rapid damage assessment and readily available replacement components. Third, survivability refers to the ability to maintain some basic level of electrical functionality to individual consumers and communities in the event of a complete loss of electrical service from the distribution system.

Would you give us your views on how DHS can help the electricity sector focus and plan for an EMP event involving what it commonly refers to as resiliency issues which would incorporate prevention, recovery, and survivability?

Mr. BECK. Thank you for the question. I think that the position for DHS of what DHS can provide really is leadership. The DHS is not a regulatory agency. It functions by enhancing public-private

---

*The information is retained in committee files.

partnerships and information dissemination, and as such they have the ability to work across multiple sectors. They work with the first-responder community, they work with science and technology, they work with industry to provide frameworks and guidelines for all, the whole spectrum that you mentioned. That can be from protecting or mitigating equipment themselves, that can be about operational procedures, and it can also be about educating first responders and local authorities on what the situation might look like in the event of one of these events and how best to prepare for planning.

So as an example, with Superstorm Sandy, you mentioned that debris, downed lines, these kinds of things were a major problem. There was flooding, et cetera. In an EMP or GMD scenario, that particular issue will probably not be something to worry about, but there would be other planning. You mentioned the electricity crews. Well, as Dr. Frankel mentioned, with a Nation-wide footprint, there could be outages in a lot of areas, and so preparation for having electrical crews be ready for the kind of restoration that will be needed, that kind of thing I think is the area where DHS could provide the best leadership.

Ms. CLARKE. My time has lapsed, but, gentlemen, was there anything that you wanted to add to that response? Yield back.

Mr. FRANKEL. Well, I would add that the recommendations of the EMP Commission directed at the Department of Homeland Security are still kind of languishing out there, and I think they are still pretty good.

Mr. PERRY. The Chairman thanks the gentlelady for the first round anyhow, and the Chairman recognizes Representative Franks.

Mr. FRANKS. Well, thank you, Mr. Chairman.

I was struck by the last remark that you made. As you know, the Department of Homeland Security Act of 2002 stood up the Department of Homeland Security and created a Presidentially-appointed position for an assistant secretary for infrastructure protection. That is the quote. The mission is to recommend measures necessary to protect the key resources and critical infrastructure of the United States in coordination with other agencies of the Federal Government, but in your estimation you are suggesting that that hasn't been fulfilled. Do you think that passing this Critical Infrastructure Protection Act would catalyze some change in that direction? I will pass that to you, Dr. Frankel, and if anyone else wants to address it.

Mr. FRANKEL. I absolutely do think that that is almost a necessary first step. Now, you mentioned the Department of Homeland Security was stood up in 2002 or 2003. It was actually stood up after the legislation which created the EMP Commission, and, as such, only the Secretary of Defense was mandated to actually take a look and respond. He could have rejected them, or, as it turned out, he looked at them and accepted them, but there was no such, you know, belly button identified within the Department of Homeland Security, which, of course, didn't exist at the time, and so it was hard to find anybody who owned the problem.

There indeed was an assistant for infrastructure protection. In fact, I believe I recall going in with Dr. Graham and briefing him, or perhaps General Lawson, and—but nevertheless, you know, kind-of the ripples died out, and there is no detectable resonance these days.

Mr. FRANKS. Well, the military seems to get it. I mean, it doesn't seem to be a fact—I have heard, in the very highest echelons of our military command in the United States, them deem this or term this cybersecurity and EMP as kissing cousins because they affect the same networks, and because in a sense EMP is like an ultimate cybersecurity threat because if you have no electricity, you have no networks.

But with that said, NERC is currently undergoing a rulemaking procedure to look at protecting the grid from GMD, not so much EMP yet, and from my vantage point it appears that they may be using some faulty science or data that justify inadequate standards that, in my judgment, don't go far enough. It also appears that the standard may include only procedural and operational changes, and it leaves, in my judgment, our citizens at risk.

It appears to me that hardware-based solutions eliminate, to a large extent, the worst of the most catastrophic element that might happen here. Can you tell me and this committee the importance of using hardware-based solutions versus just procedural methods to protect just against vulnerabilities? I would like to start over here with Dr. Pry and go through the group here, because I may not have another opportunity.

Mr. PRY. Before answering that question, I would like to add that, you know, the Critical Infrastructure Protection Act is provisioned to establish a scenario focused on EMP. A National planning scenario on EMP was one of the core recommendations of the EMP Commission, so that legislation would be realizing this long-delayed goal of the Commission.

A hardware-based solution to this is absolutely necessary. Operational procedures alone are not going to work against either a geomagnetic disturbance or—and certainly not against a nuclear EMP attack. The United States—well, not the United States, NERC, but the NERC, the North American Electric Reliability Corporation, has been resisting that and trying to argue that operational procedures would be sufficient for dealing with a geomagnetic storm, a Carrington-class geomagnetic storm, and frankly it has been junk science.

I know this and can say this because I have been on their Geomagnetic Disturbance Task Force, and other members of my task force are still on the NERC Geomagnetic Disturbance Task Force. They can't keep us off it. Under the law they have to allow outside independent observers, and we have been able to watch that process and see the junk science process in action where they basically cook the books to try to convince people that operational procedures will suffice.

The most notorious example of this was the NERC's 2012 report that asserted that if a Carrington-class geomagnetic superstorm happened today, that they would be able to recover the grid in 24 hours, and then weeks after they delivered that report, we had a weather event sweep through Washington, DC, that caused a black-out of large parts of the area that lasted more than a week, you know, which showed that they can't even cope using operational procedures with normal terrestrial weather, let alone an unprecedented thing like a Carrington Event.

Moreover, our closest NATO allies in the United Kingdom, who are also very concerned about this, within a few weeks of the NERC 2012 report coming out put out their own report that also assessed that they had to harden their grid because operational procedures alone wouldn't be sufficient to protect against either a natural or nuclear EMP.

You know, NERC stands alone in this belief among all the studies that have been done by the U.S. Government and even by our allies that operational procedures will suffice, and, you know, I think we are just seeing the same old story again where industry will do whatever it can to resist having to spend the money on the hardware, just like the cigarette industry, just like I like to think of the zeppelin industry in the 1920s that convinced everybody, you know, that travel by hydrogen balloon was safe, that they could use operational procedures to make zeppelin travel safe even though helium was available and it would cost a little more to use it, and in effect NERC has got us all on the Hindenburg, and we are flying toward a rendezvous with a geomagnetic catastrophe in the future.

Mr. FRANKS. Thank you, Mr. Chairman. I don't know if the others had any response. I know I am certainly out of time. Yield back.

Mr. PERRY. If you ask the question, the others can respond.

Mr. FRANKEL. I concur with Dr. Pry that hardware solutions are, indeed, called for. I am not as familiar with the specific studies that he is referring to, but it is my impression that we have a problem of overfamiliarity, if you will, for the NERC. This is a well-known physics phenomenon, the inducing of these currents by these geomagnetic storms, and the power industry has known about this pretty much forever. They have procedures and things in place to prevent that sort of thing, and I think they are just a tad too comfortable with their ability to deal with this thing, and the thing that we are now talking about is the possibility that will be of an intensity that they simply have not prepared for. Yes, it is low frequency, but it is very high probability—I think I said 100 percent before—that it will happen at some point, scale it on the 100-year scale. I think they are not willing to go that—like, yes, they know about geomagnetic storms; yes, they have indeed protected against geomagnetic storms, but they haven't really taken that final step to protect against the kind of the super-Katrina kind-of analogue, and I feel that is what we are faced with here.

Mr. BECK. I would just comment that FERC Order 779 is a two-phase approach where the first phase was operational measures, and the second phase had to do with the more detailed analysis up to and including hardware-based solutions. The trade-off is one basically of complication and ability to respond in a timely manner.

Operational procedures may be effective in a manageable-sized geomagnetic disturbance when there is decent warning, which may be available if the storm is slow moving. For massive solar storms, typically the velocity is higher; the warning time is less. This would really put stress on the operators as they tried to go through those procedures. But it was a place to start because it could be done immediately where there needs to be more analysis and understanding of some of the hardware-based solutions.

But ultimately a mixture would probably be best, and certainly if you include EMP, where warning time would be zero, then operational procedures would be unbelievably challenging for the operators to be able to deal with an EMP event using operational procedures alone.

Mr. PERRY. The Chairman thanks the gentlemen.

We are going to, without objection, move to the second round. I would like to start with Dr. Pry.

You mentioned in your testimony a satellite passing over the Washington-New York corridor. I would like you to describe the importance or the potential importance of that, and in that context also please describe the National electric grid interconnection, what regions of the country are most vulnerable to grid collapse as a result of EMP attack.

Mr. PRY. Well, the KSM–3 satellite was orbited by North Korea in December 2012, about 3 months before we had our gravest nuclear crisis with North Korea when in February 2012 they ignited—they conducted their third nuclear test, violating international law, and when the United States international community moved to impose additional sanctions to punish North Korea for this, they started threatening to make nuclear strikes against the United States. There was a nuclear crisis so grave during the period from February 12 through the end of April that, you know, the President was sending B–2 bombers over the demilitarized zone to do practice bombing runs and demonstration exercises; strengthened the National missile defense, including moving a THAAD interceptor to Guam just in case Kim Jong-Un tried to deliver on these nuclear threats.

In the midst of this crisis, the KSM–3, which was still orbiting, its orbit followed the exact orbit that the Soviets had come up with in the Cold War for a secret nuclear weapon to conduct a surprise nuclear attack called a fractional orbital bombardment system. It is basically a space launch vehicle that uses a nuclear weapon disguised as a satellite, and instead of launching over the North Pole and following a normal ballistic trajectory toward the United States, it launches south and crosses over the south polar region and comes up from—approaches from the south because we don't have any ballistic missile early warning radars in that location or interceptors, and we are blind to the south and defenseless, and so you would be able to detonate a warhead and do an EMP attack and catch us by surprise. That was the plan during the Cold War, and the trajectory and the altitude of this satellite were precisely the same as the kinds of fobs that the Soviets had used.

Between April 8 and the 16th of April, it went from the center of the United States, and on the 16th was passing over the Washington, DC/New York corridor, which is the ideal location for putting down a peak field, because if you look at where our EHV transformers are located, they are most deeply located, the largest numbers of them, the map is just almost a solid block of red because it is so densely concentrated, the EHV transformers in that area. If you wanted to take down the eastern grid, that would be the best place to place a peak EMP field. Taking out the eastern grid is really all you have to do because 75 percent of our power is generated in the eastern grid. The western grid is the next most important, and the Texas grid is the third most important. But that was the KSM–3 threat and its relationship to the grid system.

Mr. PERRY. Thank you.

Speaking of those, the transformers, it has been noted that the Extremely High-Voltage, the EHV transformers which are indispensable to the electric grid, are expensive and hard to replace. If you know, what is the lead time for manufacturing new or replacement transformers, and given that there are limited manufacturers in the United States, where are the suppliers located?

Mr. PRY. There are two places that manufacture these for export, South Korea and Germany, and we are still dependent on them. I know there is a DHS briefing going around that says we have limited capabilities to manufacture EHV transformers in the United States. In fact, we currently don't really have demonstrated capability to manufacture these transformers in the United States yet. They have to be made by hand the way they were made back in Nikola Tesla's day, the inventor of the EHV transformer.

So every one is custom made, every one has a unique role to play in the grid. They aren't mass produced. It is not easy. There is a lot of—they have to be custom made, and there is a lot of artisanship, as it were, that goes into the making of these transformers. Brazil tried to become independent of making its own EHV transformers, oh, maybe a decade ago, and it took them 5 years before they were able to start attempting to make their first transformers, and they didn't perform well. So now Brazil gave up on that, and it has to import them.

So it remains to be seen if the United States can actually manufacture any of its own EHV transformers yet. We haven't manufactured one and put them out in the field and seen if they last and stand up to this. It takes 18 months under normal conditions to build one of these transformers.

Mr. PERRY. Has the United States ever manufactured them, or is it something that we did and then got out of?

Mr. PRY. We did. We invented them. We invented all of the technology that goes into the electric grid, you know, back near the turn of the century. Nikola Tesla. The first electric grid in the world was up near Niagara Falls, the first hydroelectric station, and the thing that makes the grid possible, the cornerstone of our modern civilization, is the EHV transformer invented by Nikola Tesla because it makes it possible to take power from a place like Niagara Falls and project it long distances, down to New York City, for example. Then there is another transformer at the end of the line that steps it down so it can be used locally. But like so many things that we invented and we used to manufacture and exported to the world, we don't make it here anymore.

Mr. PERRY. The Chairman's time has expired.

Recognize the Ranking Member.

Ms. CLARKE. Thank you, Mr. Chairman.

I just wanted to add to the DHS question that I had raised earlier that one of the observations of the Sandy event was the unintended consequence of the grid going—the electricity going out was that people forgot that fuel stations are run through—by electricity, and so we ended up having a fuel crisis at the same time.

So there is sort of a collateral damage piece to this that I hope is acknowledged as we go through this discussion about what happens in areas when just in a short period of time electrical shortages occur or the grid goes out, because even if you were trying to move physical assets, if you don't prepare for things like fuel stations that are run by electricity, you will have a massive issue.

Dr. Beck, I wanted to talk about the international nature of what we are talking about here, because your report speaks to that, and I know in your London conference on grid security last year, there were representatives from business and industry in addition to governments. Could you describe the conversations and discussions about how the insurance industry is viewing EMP and geomagnetic disturbances in the electric industry?

Mr. BECK. Yes. The past Washington summit was a first meeting of what we called the three-sector roundtable, which was the electric power sector, Government, and the insurance industry representatives, that met to try to talk through some of these issues about how they might be addressed.

The insurance sector has long been the sector with the most expertise on risk analysis, which is basically what they do and how they develop their products. It is difficult in occurrences like this where the typical traditional risk analysis method is to use an actuarial method where you have a large database of previous events, and you can look at probabilities over time. It becomes much more difficult to do that when you have events like a large geomagnetic storm that don't occur very often and haven't—very large storms have not occurred during the time that we have had a ubiquitous and electric grid.

So that is a challenge, but it is—and those discussions are ongoing. It is a difficult question to address, but it is very encouraging that those discussions have begun, and that they are getting input from the electric power sector, from governments. It is a way perhaps beyond or in addition to a regulatory approach that could incentivize the industry. It could provide a business case or a cost mechanism, as the insurance industry has done in other industries, for example with fire codes. Fire insurance, you can get a better deal on your fire insurance if you have a sprinkler system. Well, perhaps an electric utility could get a better deal on their insurance, have they done engineering analysis on their system on what their GMD vulnerability is, for example.

As I said, those are on-going discussions that are in their early stages, and so I don't have any specifics on. There aren't recommendations yet, but that kind of approach where you have the insurance sector playing a role and paying attention to this—you know, this threat is, I think, a very encouraging sign.

Ms. CLARKE. How do you plan to propose international standards if there are so many different individualized systems that need specialized mitigation? I mean, just another case in point, when there was a major Northeast corridor blackout, and it originated actually in Canada and then came all the way down and took out New York City, you know. How do we look at the differences and come up with the specialized mitigation?

Mr. BECK. Good question. Basically, so first of all, you are absolutely right, the report that you mentioned earlier, EIS Council did a survey of 11 countries, their different experiences with geomagnetic disturbances principally, but also EMP, and their different approaches, which were a mixture of hardware and procedural approaches, and from that I would say you are correct that each country has a unique grid, but there are lots of similarities in that the physics of electric transmission generation is the same. So you have transformers, you have generators, you have transmission assets, you have generation assets, and you have loads.

Those are the same everywhere, so while any specific mitigation method—for example, Finland has a very robust grid, and they don't really use operational procedures; they are all hardware-based. So they have very tough transformers. They compensate their long transmission lines with series capacitors which have an ancillary benefit of blocking currents. They use special reactors to ground that have a resistance that dampen currents that come in. So they have a very robust system based on hardware solutions.

Another example of that is New Zealand that uses grounding resistors to protect some of their transformers. Other countries, including the United Kingdom, a mixture of some of the other Scandinavian countries use a more blended approach of procedural and hardware solutions.

So I wouldn't say—I think standards are excellent in—for example, used by the International Electrotechnical Commission or the IEEE that put out recommended standards for certain types of performance and parameters through—under which these components should operate safely, and that gives the industry something to guide on. But it is, I think, more of a question of information sharing so that there is a suite of options out there that are tested and peer reviewed that can then be used by the industry or by governments, et cetera, to address the problem.

Ms. CLARKE. Thank you, Mr. Chairman. I yield back.

Mr. PERRY. The Chairman thanks the gentlelady.

The Chairman recognizes Representative Franks.

Mr. FRANKS. Well, thank you, Mr. Chairman. Thank you for your forbearance and just the privilege you have given me to be on the dais here today.

I just have two remaining questions really, and, Dr. Pry, just a quick response here. I know a lot of us as we consider this issue, we realize that if indeed we did lose our grid, in a worst-case scenario, and we are not projecting a worst-case scenario, but if it did happen, really the aftermath where society would begin to tear ourselves apart seems to be the most frightening aspect of it to me. So the cost of doing nothing is significantly high, and I think you have demonstrated that well, but could you give us a sense of how expensive it would be to harden our bulk power system enough to recover from a major event; in other words, where we keep our main components intact, and we can bring our grid back on-line? I have been told that a couple, $3 billion over 5 years might do it, and that might be less than $1 per year per ratepayer. Am I accurately expressing that?

Mr. PRY. Yes. In fact, your estimate is high compared to the Congressional EMP Commission's estimate, which was that it would cost about $2 billion over 3 to 5 years to harden the bulk power system, and $10–20 billion over that same period, you know, would protect all of the critical infrastructures.

The U.S. Federal Energy Regulatory Commission put out an estimate in 2010, in its 2010 report, that it could be paid for by—it would increase the rate, the average ratepayer's electric bill. Your annual electric bill would be increased by 20 cents annually amortized over a period of years, so you would hardly even feel the pain, you know, that way.

It is not necessary—in addition to the cost of hardening the country, perhaps we should also keep in mind the cost to States, because while the preferred solution, of course, is to do this Nationally, the Commission noted that it is possible for a State to island its grid, and some States are planning to do exactly that because they are so frustrated that Washington has not taken any steps since 2008 and the Commission delivery of its report.

As I said last year, it has only taken a year for Maine to pass a bill. Virginia did so earlier this year, and Florida is working on passing the bill now to island its State, you know, in a State grid. I think that this is a germane example. North Carolina is interested in islanding its grid, and they are considering legislation as well. It would probably—it would cost something like $5–10 million to harden the whole State of North Carolina, which is less than what we are spending on a program in the Department of Defense called SPIDERS, which is spending $30 million to——

Mr. FRANKS. You said $5–10 million, correct?

Mr. PRY. Five to ten million dollars for the State of North Carolina, which has six military bases in it, okay? The SPIDERS program from the Department of Defense is spending $30 million to provide energy security for just three military bases.

Mr. FRANKS. Well, that was the main point I was making was that, you know, when we were in Israel, some of us—in fact, some of you on the panel and I were in Israel about a year-and-a-half ago; I just returned from Israel. They—to use their terminology, they consider this a very attractive problem—and this is just to show you how the Israelis deal with these things—they said, because it represents something that is very dangerous, but very, very—something that can be addressed with reasonable cost.

Mr. PRY. Yes.

Mr. FRANKS. So they are moving forward in a very significant way.

My last question, Mr. Chairman, it goes to all of them, and I will start down here with you, Mr. Beck. At present it is not really clear who is in charge of protecting the Nation against solar and nuclear EMP or IEMI. Would you be in favor of DHS taking the role? If not, who should do it? If you can each articulate briefly who you think should take the lead on this, what do you think really this represents to America in terms of threat and danger, how serious is it, what keeps you up, and what is the next step?

Mr. BECK. Thank you. You saved the easy question for last, which is nice.

Well, the U.S. electric grid is the most complicated in the world both by physical design; by the overlapping regulatory authority,

50 States, a Federal Government, 3,500 electric companies, et cetera.

When we did the international study, it was pretty easy, and one of the things where lessons learned was easy was because you could look at Finland, which has one company and one regulator, right? So a much easier thing to deal with. Here it is—that does make it very difficult, and so I have to—in all honesty, and not to try to duck the question, but the answer is somewhat complicated because there are all these agencies, and there isn't just one agency that is in charge.

So I do think it makes sense, especially in the discussion that we are having before this committee, that DHS plays a major role because of, I think, the vast utility in addressing this issue through infrastructure protection. We talked about DOD can't do it, it is not—at least certainly the solar threat, there is no deterrence possible, et cetera. So leading from an infrastructure protection standpoint is very important, and then the structures then that flow from that where you have the Department of Energy and Federal Energy Regulatory Commission as the sector-specific agencies, that can make sense, but it certainly has to be done in coordination with the State-level governments as well.

Mr. FRANKEL. Yes, certainly the Department of Homeland Security, I think, has the primary responsibility, but we should also not forget the Department of Energy. They have offices of energy assurance, and they should also be playing some role. Right now I don't discern exactly what it is, but somewhere between those two, with DHS in the primary role, I think that is where you look for leadership.

I want to at least mention the Department of Defense not in a leadership role in this instance, but they are doing a lot of relevant work developing hardening techniques. Worried about their own networks and things of that sort, but they have very important technology support to contribute to that sort of thing. But in the end it is not their responsibility, and it is not their mission, and they are not going to do it. You need to look at those two Departments for leadership.

Mr. PRY. I agree with what has been said. The Department of Homeland Security, especially when you are looking at the role from the Critical Infrastructure Protection Act for planning, training, and resource allocation for emergency planners and responders—under the Department of Homeland Security, within the Department of Homeland Security, the logical regulatory authority to work most closely over the electric grid should be the U.S. Federal Energy Regulatory Commission, the U.S. FERC, and this would be addressed by the SHIELD Act that Mr. Franks is sponsoring in front of the House Energy and Commerce Committee.

I think this is really like the—almost equally important with the Critical Infrastructure Protection Act in terms of its passage, because the reality and the reason we have this problem is because the electric power industry exists in a 19th Century regulatory environment. I mean, there is no Federal agency that has the kind of regulatory authority relative to the electric power industry that, for example, the Federal Aviation Administration has over the airline industry, you know. I think all Americans and even Tea Party

Republicans would agree that, you know, we need an FAA so you have independent inspectors who will go out and see, you know, is there metal fatigue in the wings of this aircraft, and when that airplane can't fly, and that if an airplane crashes, you have an FAA to inspect the crash and find out what happened so that it never happens again. We do this because hundreds of lives are at stake, and we need to maintain the public safety. That is why we have an FAA.

But the U.S. FERC doesn't have that power. It can ask the NERC, which represents the industry, and previously was a trade association, by the way, and unofficially is a lobby for the electric power industry, and NERC is the one that is in charge. They regulate themselves through the NERC. The FERC can ask them to come up with a plan.

I mean, here is a great example is the great 2003 Northeast blackout was caused by a falling tree branch that caused cascading—it took them 10 years for NERC to come up with a plan, vegetation management plan. So not just—you know, cyber 5 years; they were asked for a plan some 5 years before they started moving on that.

So U.S. FERC, I say, would be the tip of the spear for dealing with the electric power industry.

Mr. FRANKS. Mr. Chairman, thank you so very much for your forbearance, and thank you for the opportunity here today, and thank all of you.

Mr. PERRY. Ladies and gentlemen, votes have been called. I want to thank the witnesses for their valuable testimony and the Members for their questions. The Members of the committee may have some additional questions, and if they do, we ask that you submit them in writing and so there can be responses.

Without objection, the subcommittee stands adjourned.

[Whereupon, at 3:25 p.m., the subcommittee was adjourned.]

○